Managing Service as a Strategic Profit Center

Donald F. Blumberg
President
D. F. Blumberg & Associates, Inc.

McGraw-Hill, Inc.

New York   St. Louis   San Francisco   Auckland   Bogotá
Caracas   Hamburg   Lisbon   London   Madrid
Mexico   Milan   Montreal   New Delhi   Paris
San Juan   São Paulo   Singapore
Sydney   Tokyo   Toronto

*To Sara Blumberg, Yetta T., Mike and Susan,
and especially Judy, my wife, whose support
provided the incentive and encouragement
for the completion of this book.*

Library of Congress Cataloging-in-Publication Data
Blumberg, Donald F.
  Managing service as a strategic profit center / Donald F.
  Blumberg.
    p. cm.
  Includes bibliographical references.
  ISBN 0-07-006189-0
  1. Customer service—Management.   2. Strategic planning.
  I. Title
  HF5415.5.B57   1991   90-5797
  658.8′12—dc20   CIP

1 2 3 4 5 6 7 8 9 0   DOC/DOC   9 5 4 3 2 1 0

ISBN 0-07-006189-0

*The sponsoring editor for this book was Barbara B. Toniolo, the editing
supervisor was Laura Givner, the designer was Naomi Auerbach, and the
production supervisor was Suzanne W. Babeuf. It was set in Baskerville by
McGraw-Hill's Professional and Reference Division composition unit.*

Printed and bound by R. R. Donnelley & Sons Company.

For information about our audio products, write us at:
Newbridge Book Clubs, 3000 Cindel Drive, Delran, NJ 08370

Contents

Preface

Service, if strategically managed, directed, and controlled, can be a major source of revenue and profits—as well as the critical factor in the successful growth of a company. Research suggests that profit margins for services are about 15 to 25 percent before taxes, whereas those for products are typically 7 to 11 percent. Return on investment in the service sector is in the vicinity of 70 to 80 percent, allowing investment recovery in under a year in some cases. An in-depth analysis of more than 250 companies reveals that anywhere from 25 to 40 percent of corporate revenues and from 20 to 50 percent of corporate profits can be generated from the service component of a business—particularly if service is run as a line of business or strategic profit center.

In this book you will find a step-by-step explanation of how to develop and plan the service organization as a strategic line of your business— how to market service, price service, manage and control service operations, and use advanced systems and technology to improve service operations and productivity. Here is a complete prescription for managing service as a successful profit center—not just as an adjunct of a product business or a general attempt to keep customers satisfied.

Based on more than 20 years of experience in the service market, *Managing Service as a Strategic Profit Center* provides both the underlying theory and the specific recommendations for strategic action that can lead to the development of new revenues, new businesses, higher profitability, new products, and new levels of market differentiation.

Donald F. Blumberg

Acknowledgments

This effort was based on the results of more than 25 years of management consulting in the service field. I owe a debt of gratitude to the staff of Decision Sciences Corporation and D. F. Blumberg & Associates, Inc., particularly Bill Pollock, who helped in developing the research data, and Gaby Shaw, managing director of Blumberg Shaw Consulting in the United Kingdom. The many service executives with whom I have worked—including Dave Daley at Bull, Bruce Jacobs at Burnup and Sims, Bill Thompson and Tom Quinn of Western Union, Bill Fitzgerald at Control Data, Jim Maloney at Coca-Cola, Carlton Smith at Harris, Ron Janusz at Xerox and NEC, Earl Humphrey at Tandem, Tom Bartlett at Bell Atlantic Customer Service, and Al Luft at Dupont—have provided much insight and "real-world" rules of thumb. Finally, my thanks go to the Association of Field Service Managers International (AFSMI), the National Association of Service Managers (NASM), and the editors of *Service News Magazine* and *Microservice Management Magazine* for both encouragement and the use of their "platform" to present many of the views discussed in this book.

As usual, the credit belongs to many; complaints, critiques, and suggestions should be directed to me.

Donald F. Blumberg

1

A Strategic View of Service

Service—More Than Just a Way of Dealing with Customers

The continuing growth of the service sector of the economy, combined with increasing global competition, is placing greater focus on the general concept of service as a strategic line of business. We have always produced, sold, and used both goods and services. Traditional services such as banking, health care, retail trade, restaurants and other food services, accounting, and legal and other professional services have always been part of the economy. Technology and products also require service and support. It is increasingly clear that both the growth in technology and new marketing and distribution concepts of the "traditional service" market have provided a significant new framework in which to strategically manage, plan, and control both the "traditional" services and the newly emerging market requirements and opportunities for technology service and support. There has, of course, always been a general recognition of the importance of service to the customer in every business and the need for managing the customer-service interface. However, the concept of a *strategic* approach to management, marketing, control, and direction of service as a full, profitable line of business has rarely been examined in a context other than a specific service industry or company situation.

A broad and increasing array of new service concepts and innovations is now being developed and profitably implemented in the market. Domino Pizza's use of delivery as a service differentiation mechanism in the fast-food industry, IBM's strategic use of total service and support as a primary mechanism in maintaining market share and control in the

1

computer industry, and Citibank's electronic banking technology, designed to significantly improve funds transfer services to both businesses and consumers, are just a few examples of both the growing focus on service as a business opportunity and the strategic use of service in generating substantial revenues and profits.

In these situations and others the delivery of *service* is more than just a mechanism for dealing with customers; it is *the* strategic competitive advantage. The marketplace perception is that IBM provides a strategic commitment to full service and support on a timely and responsive basis. This feeling of assurance that "one cannot go wrong by dealing with IBM" because it provides quality *services* in a timely and responsive manner makes it possible for IBM not only to gain and control market share in its markets but also to charge a *substantial premium* (more than what other directly competitive vendors charge) for, in effect, its service strategy. IBM has many product competitors, some of which offer better technology at lower prices; however, it has been and still is today a leader in service and support, and that, to a major extent, has made the real difference. In effect, at IBM service is managed and controlled, delivered and marketed strategically. In this sense, service is *as* important as, if not *more* important than, individual product lines. IBM is not the only firm using and managing service strategically. Many other firms in other markets have also recognized the value of a total service commitment, either as part of a total product and service offering or as an independent line of business. This book focuses on such a global and total approach to service and the ways to manage service strategically.

Service strategy is critical to the whole business; it is not just an element of individual product lines. This use of service in a strategic sense can be found in a wide variety of businesses and markets (both for products and for services). The use of strategic service can create a major—in fact, unique—differentiation for new and existing businesses, revise and give new light to existing businesses, and create new, entirely different businesses. In fact, the growing service economy and the general maturing of both the product technology and consumers are increasing the demand for *innovative strategic services* and a broader array of services designed to meet the *total* service and support needs and requirements of customers. The new shop-at-home services using cable television as a delivery mechanism are only one example of such new strategic services.

The Traditional Approach to Service—Conventional Wisdom

However, even within the context of these obvious examples and emerging opportunities, service still tends to be viewed tactically, and without much enthusiasm. Conventional wisdom is that *products* are more important than service and that service is, in general, not very profitable, since it is *labor-intensive* and *lacks economies of scale*. Service to the customer is often viewed as a necessary evil; keep the customer happy through a positive approach, courtesy, and a willingness to serve, so long as it can be done within a fixed budget. Perhaps the greatest problem is the fact that our entire strategic management philosophy tends to *presume the existence of and focus on* the *product*, or *tangible goods*, elements of the business. We tend to think of business in product terms, and our financial and accounting systems tend to measure revenue, costs, and profit by product line. This is true both for product-manufacturing firms (where the product or technology defines the strategic business unit) and for service businesses where the product involved in the service tends to become the major area of focus. For example, "steak house" versus Italian food is used to differentiate restaurants, just as retail stores tend to focus on the product lines they sell. We often neglect or ignore the already existing large and rapidly growing service opportunities and service market demand because of our focus on the product and our inability to relate directly to service requirements and needs of the market. Most managers have not been trained to take a *comprehensive approach* to service in which management of service is based upon the specific and unique characteristics of the *service* business rather than treated as a subset or specialized version of a product or product business.

Obviously, providing service for customers is important. Businesses cannot ignore customers. But a full-service approach, particularly in a maturing economy, can be the critical difference in success. This book demonstrates how a change in the conventional view of service as a tactical element of the product business to a view of service *as a full strategy* can pay off in the marketplace. In fact, service *should* be viewed and managed as a profit center and a key element of the business.

What Is Strategic Service?

On the basis of my extensive experience—more than 20 years of consulting work in developing strategies and tactics for service-based businesses—I believe that great opportunities exist in service. A strategic approach to service can generate significant revenues and profits directly, as well as other associated values of critical interest in the market. This concept of *strategic service* is based upon viewing present and emerging service requirements and needs of customers as a market of its own, which can be optimally served and supported to generate substantial profits and return on investment. The basic thesis is that this service opportunity is just as important as, if not *more* important than, product-opportunities, and such service opportunities should be pursued strategically. In fact, by separating and focusing on service to the customer as a line of business, it is possible both to optimize customer satisfaction and profitability from the service provided and to provide the required support to the product, if one exists or needs to exist.

Equally important in the strategic service concept is the need to recognize that there are clear and important differences between the optimum strategies for managing intangible services as a business and those for managing the tangible product business. These factors include managing the ability and time to serve, as well as the actual service performance. This idea is developed more thoroughly during the course of this book.

I believe that the strategic service approach can be used for *both* traditional or stand-alone service businesses and services emerging from product lines of business where the product technology often hides or masks the service opportunities.

Customer Service versus Field Service

In developing the philosophy of *strategic service* for profit, I must first define the terms of reference. There are usually two types of "service" concepts that are often utilized interchangeably but are, nevertheless, very different in terms of the strategic service philosophy. Presales activities—including alerting the potential customer to new offerings, contacting the potential customer to determine interest in new products and/or services (i.e., telemarketing), and interacting with a customer before the actual sale through advertising, sales promotion, etc.—are, of course, services. They are, however, a part of the general marketing function found in any business. While clearly any examination of business opportunity will involve this type of presales "service," I will be speaking about service from the standpoint of satisfying the intangible-goods, or nongoods, demands and requirements of a customer base. The focus is on the business of delivering services either independently or in conjunction with a tangible product. I thus use *service* in the global sense and not in the narrow terms of the personal interaction with a potential customer *prior* to a sale or as part of the general selling process. Thus customer-related presales service (i.e., those interactions provided prior to the actual sale) is viewed as a *part* of the overall customer service and field, or after-sale, service business equation (Table 1-1).

An important difference between products and services is that service is often utilized during the sales process. In restaurant service, for example, the waiter delivers the food; the customer consumes it. The completion of the process constitutes the full sale of the service. In service the customer is often directly involved in the service delivery and

Table 1-1. Customer Service and Field Service Definitions

Activity	Function
General customer service and coordination	Managing the general customer-service interface
Customer assistance and service prior to the sale	Identifying the products and/or services available Alerting the customer to new products and/or services Determining customer interest in new products and/or services (telemarketing) Providing information on products and/or services: 　Form, fit, function 　Applicability 　Price
Customer and field service after the sale	Reporting complaints and issues related to the sale and/or delivery
Field service after the sale	Delivering and/or installing the product or service Managing the warranty process and period Providing maintenance and repair—corrective action Providing related services or products: 　Parts 　Software 　Consultation 　Training

use process. As an example, banking services require some action by the customer to both initiate a transaction and close it out. The bank teller is involved with the customer in the process of cashing a check. In general, for products there is a very specific transition between customer service before the sale and field service after the sale. For service, this distinction (between before-sale customer service and after-sale field service) is not as clear. We must clearly define this transition point in order to manage and control service effectively.

Service Transition Point—Service before and after the Sale

The critical *transition point* between the *customer service activity* regarding the initial sale and the *field service activity* which relates to recording and dealing with problems or complaints and related issues after the sale or delivery of the product or service must be managed. I have chosen to consider this as part of the *general field service,* or *after-sale service,* activity. Clearly, the general coordination of all services to the customer (both the before-sale customer service and the after-sale field service) needs to be managed and controlled. We need to view the individual customer's and market's need for all services as one integrated package or portfolio (of service needs), not separated by presales or postsales issues. This is best accomplished by:

1. Recording and noting the customer's identification and characteristics at the time of the initial sale

2. Clearly describing to the customer the services and support to be provided at the time of sale

3. Providing an easy and simple process for the customer to report a problem or complaint, in the event that the service is not provided

4. Communicating to the customer at the time of sale the contact point for this process

5. Following through on problems or complaints reported to ensure that they were handled and/or corrected to the satisfaction of the customer

It is at this transition point where the service person–customer interface is most crucial. How the service person appears and what he or she says or does at the point of sale create the initial bond between the customer and the organization and establish the continuing relationships upon which both the actual service delivery and performance and the perception of service performance will be built. It is, therefore, critical to both define and prescribe this interface and ensure, through training, sensitivity, awareness, and incentives, that this initial and continuing bond is forged.

The service sales and customer interface person, as the first contact with the customer, will initiate the perception process. Thus it is essential that this key representative of the organization:

- Show strong customer *sensitivity* and *awareness*
- Understand the dimensions of the service portfolio to be offered to the customer
- Deliver the customer interface service on a friendly, committed, proactive basis
- Be aware of the need for continuing feedback on delivered service performance
- Provide the customer with a clear method for reporting on problems, complaints, or new service needs and requirements

This should be achieved through positive organizational action and reinforcement to:

- Provide specific procedures, policies, and objectives for customer service interface and action, through training
- Monitor, coordinate, and evaluate performance against policy and plan

Nothing could be more damaging to the service organization–customer relationship than customer service personnel who are passive or insensitive toward the customer requesting and needing services. Waiting in line in a restaurant or bank while the customer service personnel talk among themselves or ignore the service queue or waiting for a service organization to answer the phone can be downright irritating, if not a complete turnoff. Slow or inaccurate service by waiters in a restaurant, attendants in a service station, or salesclerks in a retail store indicates to the customer that the service organization is uncaring and unsympathetic to service; poor service also generates a highly negative perception of service commitment or quality.

The key steps in achieving an optimum customer-service interface and transition for the customer service personnel are as follows:

- *Establish* the service interface standards or procedures, behavior, and appearance required.
- *Provide* a particular focus on *service time targets*; define how long

customers should wait and/or how long service should take, for each class or segment of customers served by each service person.

- *Provide clear-cut* incentives and performance review standards.
- *Follow up* and provide visible performance *incentives* for best service performance.

These steps should be implemented regardless of whether the product or service is an inexpensive or big-ticket item; however, the larger and more complex or critical the product or service is, the more formal and structured the transition management process needs to be.

Special Service Issues Involved in Product versus Service Sale

In developing the strategic service concept, we must also recognize that the service firm differs from the product firm in terms of interaction with the customer order under presale and postsale conditions. In the product firm, delivery is provided in terms of individual, separable, physical goods. Prior to the sale the customer can see and even touch the product. The product can be kept in stock to be ready and available in advance of the customer's needs.

In the service firm, however, services are intangible and cannot be stored. Service delivery may be continuous or separable, but it specifically involves both *actual performance* and the *ability to perform* (i.e., timely response). This "ability to perform a service" is a *critical component* which leads to important differences with respect to both customer perception and time criticality and sensitivity that are not generally found in product businesses. In service, since the product cannot be stored or inventoried and cannot be seen or "touched," the service "product" is largely defined in terms of *perception*—particularly customer or market perceptions of time and the confidence that the service can and will be delivered within the time frame required by the customer. Since these times vary, we will see that the service "product" will have different values for one class of customer versus another. Thus the service must be defined and delivered in terms of customer segment requirements and needs, whereas the product tends to define the customer.

By focusing on service performance described in terms of both perceptions and requirements, it is possible to easily create new services for customers. The tangible and fixed product cannot be easily or quickly modified. We must define the product and then search for customers. Obviously, we can use market studies to develop an optimum match between customers' needs and requirements on the one hand and service needs on the other. The fact is that we can much more easily change the service to meet the customer's needs by changing service performance as well as perception. This ability to modify and improve the service package is not easily transferred to tangible products.

Outline of the Key Strategic Service Concepts

Now that I have identified the key factors which define the need to examine service strategically as a separate profit-based line of business, it is necessary to examine the underlying framework of the new strategic service approach. The basic framework of *strategic service* involves six key concepts:

1. *The service opportunity is significant in terms of both value and worth.* Service by itself is a great opportunity and can produce high revenue and profits over the general life cycle of a product.

2. *Service can be used to add value to tangible products.* A strategic focus on service elements added to products can create additional value for the customer.

3. *Products generate service needs.* Every product includes and/or generates service requirements.

4. *Service is governed primarily by the customer's perception of time.* Therefore, customers' perceptions of time must be used to determine service levels, requirements, and needs.

5. *Service pricing is different from product pricing.* Service price is largely determined by the *value in use* to the customer rather than the cost of service.

6. *Service must be totally managed, delivered, and controlled just like a product line of business.* But in addition, special emphasis must be placed on the key service time parameters and factors related to time.

In developing these ideas in this book, I will provide a structural framework for examining the concept of strategic service. I will examine the opportunity which it offers to make profits in the general market in traditional services and in high-tech markets, as well as opportunities for new and innovative service-based activities. I will show that this global, integrated view of service as a strategic line of business rather than just simply support to the customer can create major value by:

- Directly influencing sales
- Generating revenue and profits
- Providing market control and brand and customer loyalty

Each of these ideas is discussed below.

Service Opportunity in the Life Cycle

Service markets are growing rapidly and dynamically, driven by a number of dimensions, including (1) new technologies for delivering service, (2) the maturity and expansion of the industrial and consumer base, (3) competition, and (4) deregulation of many of the traditional service businesses (i.e., banking, transportation, communications). In addition to the demands for standard, or product-based, services, I see a significant increase in the growth of knowledge-based services: new services arising from the ability to efficiently organize, disseminate, and communicate data. However, it is important to recognize that *products*, as well as service businesses per se, generate service requirements and needs. In fact, service not only is a critically important part of any *product* business but also can be *significantly more important* than the product, in terms of revenue and profitability, over the product life cycle.

Life-Cycle Patterns

It is quite clear that every product or service proceeds through a general life cycle involving, in simple terms, the *introductory* stage, the *growth* stage, and the *mature-decline* stage (Fig. 1-1). Market research indicates that the factors of importance to the buyer of a product or service, with respect to the decision to buy, *shift* over this general life cycle. Service becomes increasingly important and ultimately the critical difference. The buyer initially focuses on the form, fit, and function (the features or capabilities which define how the product or service is to be used) in the *introductory stage* of the life cycle as the primary mechanism for selecting vendors. In the growth stage, where few vendors participate, offering various product features at different prices, the overall price-performance equation determines vendor selection. The customer will usually choose the most effective and efficient product at the lowest price, taking into account service and support. In the mature, or final, stage of the life cycle, where all vendors offer a product with essentially the same form, fit, and function and prices are generally the same, service becomes the critical factor in selection.

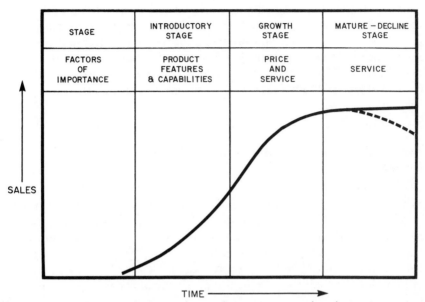

STAGE	INTRODUCTORY STAGE	GROWTH STAGE	MATURE – DECLINE STAGE
FACTORS OF IMPORTANCE	PRODUCT FEATURES & CAPABILITIES	PRICE AND SERVICE	SERVICE

SALES

TIME ⟶

Figure 1-1. Product life cycle showing factors of importance in vendor selection.

In the mature, or decline, stage of the life cycle, the only market differentiator is, in fact, the support service provided by the seller. As an example, DuPont's control of the explosives market was related much more to the array of services it provided for the buyer of explosives (i.e., "shot" planning, safety services, physical delivery) than to the product itself. In the retail field, certainly a mature business, it is the customer service support and after-sales service and delivery which make the major difference to the customer. In specific market segments (i.e., high-price buyers), the retailer which is viewed as offering the best or most comprehensive services (delivery, warranty, etc.) is usually regarded as the "best" store.

By definition, a mature industry (either product or service) occurs where there are a number of vendors producing *essentially the same item* at *stabilized or declining prices*. It should be noted that even high-tech products follow this life cycle. High-tech personal computers, for example, exhibit all the characteristics of a mature commodity-type product. Thus even for complex products, service can become the strategic selection factor for the customer. Service becomes of interest to the customer in the introductory stage, grows in importance in the growth stage, and becomes the critical factor in the mature stage.

Even for services alone, the customer service component becomes the most critical factor in market differentiation and selection. In the restaurant business, fast-food delivery—in cafeterias and diners—always existed. McDonald's defined a new level of service quality and differentiation. Banks traditionally offered the ability to exchange demand deposits for cash. Citibank and others changed the physical and time dimensions of the service through physically distributed automated teller machines (ATMs) and electronic funds transfer to offer around-the-clock, 7-day-a-week services locally to customers through their own telephones.

Service Revenues in Product Life Cycles

Clearly, in service markets such as banking, restaurants, and retail clothing, the provision of service is a major revenue source. What is not so apparent is the effect of service found in what appears (on the surface) to be a product business. An examination of the revenue stream over the life cycle of a typical product, as shown in Fig. 1-2, reveals an extremely important phenomenon: over the life cycle of product use, revenue from after-sales service of the product can become quite substantial.

Embedded within the initial purchase price of a tangible product, system, or piece of equipment are the costs of *installation and delivery services* and *initial warranty services*. Typically, these installation, delivery, and initial warranty services to the product represent 30 to 35 percent of the total initial purchase price. Every year, after the initial acceptance or warranty period, the user tends to spend approximately 20 percent of the *total* initial purchase price for maintenance and repair and re-

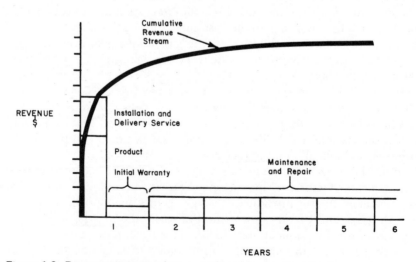

Figure 1-2. Revenue stream contribution: product versus service support.

lated support services (training, consumables, upgrades, etc.). Most products have a 5- to 7-year life cycle of use. If we multiply an average 6-year life cycle by the 20 percent per year service and support cost, for a total of 120 percent of product value, and add the 30 to 35 percent *embedded* in the initial product sale, we find that the industrial organization or consumer typically spends 150 to 155 percent of the initial tangible-product purchase price on service. Thus the typical customer spends *more than twice* the initial tangible-product price, less the cost of initially embedded services, over the life cycle of use.

In general, and particularly in high-tech markets, the product profit margins have been substantially eroding and now average about 8 to 10 percent before taxes, whereas on a fully allocated and distributed basis, service margins are high, typically averaging between 20 and 30 percent before taxes. Thus for a product business, service opportunities and requirements are much greater than the initial product sale value *over the life cycle*, in terms of both revenue and profits. When we examine the increasing installed base of products and technology and the growing dependence on that base for use by customers, we will find that the after-sales service demand market continues to grow over time and, in fact, may ultimately *exceed* the annual product sales demand (Fig. 1-3).

Most product-oriented companies fail to recognize this important change and transition and generally fail to deal with the emerging service opportunities on a strategic basis, particularly when the product's installed base has become large enough to generate a significant service revenue opportunity. This, obviously, becomes increasingly important

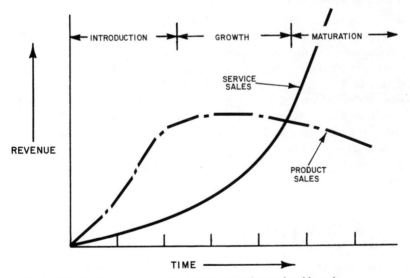

Figure 1-3. Product versus service revenues over the product life cycle.

as the product reaches the mature stage of its life cycle. Thus in the introductory stage, service tends to be viewed by the vendor as a secondary element; the major focus is usually on the new form, fit, and function of the product. But for the customer, the vendor's capability to provide service is very important. This is particularly true as the customer gains familiarity with the product and begins to use it, integrating it into daily operations.

As the product is accepted in use and becomes broadly available through several vendors, service becomes even more important to the customers as the differentiating mechanism in the decision to buy. With the growth in the installed base, this service demand can become crucial in terms of gaining and controlling market share, since increasingly, the customers will want to turn to the vendor offering the most cost-effective service relative to their needs.

Service Can Add Value

Services can add value directly to products. We have already seen that the typical product requires some services as part of its initial sales. Normally embedded in the product are services such as delivery, installation, and initial warranty. The customer's willingness to pay for these embedded services can add value to the tangible product.

Direct Added Value of Service

Services can also be used to add value directly to services. The traditional direct services such as banking and medical care provide mechanisms to improve the utilization of money, return a person's health, etc. These services all have a measurable value; additional services can be provided to add further values. To understand these values, we need to view the services from the user's perspective. Customers who are not willing to travel to a restaurant will see added value in home delivery, and customers who are not able to fit into standard clothing sizes will pay for special or custom tailoring services. Decorator services can be added to basic papering, painting, and home improvement services to add value.

Added Service Value in Extending
the Product Life Cycle

Service and support can be used to *extend* the basic product life cycle. Extended maintenance and support can give a product further use and postpone replacement. Thus the demands for service and support of products will grow over time as an economic alternative to a new capital purchase. With the new, growing product maturation in the economy, there is, therefore, an increased *interdependency* of demand between products and services, and firms that provide a strategic service portfolio can increase market control. However, this interdependency tends to move from the product to the service, particularly as the customer is faced with the question of servicing an existing product or buying a new one. For example, existing home construction will ultimately create demands for maintenance and repair services as an *alternative* to new home construction. The existing base of automobiles will generate additional maintenance and repair services as an alternative to new car purchases. This issue becomes a critical question for the vendor that provides both product and service and is interested in introducing new products. The conventional view might be to reduce service quality, increase service prices, or withhold service altogether in order to create a migration of existing customers to the new products. Firms offering services alone may, therefore, want to focus on the specific service opportunities created at the end of a product life cycle in terms of obsolete products no longer serviced by the manufacturer.

Added Value from Service in Terms of Improved Customer Satisfaction

Customer satisfaction and brand loyalty are generated by (1) providing the initial product or service on a *high-quality basis* at an effective and acceptable price and (2) providing the *customer and field service support* necessary to *guarantee* performance of the initially purchased product or service in the case of a *failure* of quality. It is, in fact, the *combination* of the product or service *quality* and the after-sale customer and field *service* that represents an extremely important equation in a number of respects. Much has been said about the need for quality in products and services—producing the best the first time. But it is essential to recognize that ultimately, the customer must perform a cost-effectiveness evaluation in making the initial purchase decision.

The Trade-Off between Service and Reliability

A customer may be neither willing nor able to pay for the *ultimate in quality*: total perfection, or zero failure to perform. In essence, customer and field service functions provide the framework in which the customer can make the trade-off between very expensive, ultrahigh reliability, in terms of quality, and the cost of after-sales support service as a substitute to ensure performance in the event of a failure to perform. The customer might be *very willing* to accept and use a less reliable and therefore less expensive product (or service) if, in the event of failure, the problem is rapidly fixed. A car which never fails over its lifetime of use might cost $1 million or more. We can easily elect to pay $20,000 for a car that fails once or twice a year, if the service to make the repair is available at a reasonable cost.

Service as an Assurance or Guarantee

Also of clear value to the customer is the comfort in knowing that the service is available when it is required. This is sometimes called "warm and fuzzies": the value to the customer in getting service *when needed*. This is a difficult concept for many vendors to understand. The supplier tends to see service demand only when the need is actually communicated by the customer and received by the vendor. But for the user, the need for service is created as soon as the requirement exists. The user has to identify the cause of the service problem, search for the agency or organization that is able to provide the required service, and contact that organization and describe the service requirement before the vendor organization is even aware of this need.

If this process is difficult or complex for the user or takes a long period of time, the user's perception of the service provided will be negatively affected. The customer should, in fact, be given a view that service is immediately available—that the service vendor is fully prepared to assist in providing full service and support, including problem identification. Steps to reduce the customer's initial concerns and increase the perception of immediate service availability and willingness to service will promote customer confidence. As an example, the availability of a 24-hour, 7-day-a-week single hot-line number for service can significantly increase the comfort level. I have always considered the Maytag advertisement showing the service man *waiting for the service call* a particularly good marketing approach, for it provides not only the image of reliability but also the strong perception of the willingness and ability to service when help is needed.

Consistency over Time

Finally, because service is a significant differentiator to the buyer or user, the highest levels of customer satisfaction or brand loyalty can be achieved through the customer or field service dimension, which is observed or used *over a long period of time*, rather than the product dimension, which primarily exists only at *the time of initial purchase*. Thus it is essential to provide a constant level of service quality over time. This *consistency* is critical added value in developing a long-term perception of quality service commitment.

In general, most managers and executives recognize the importance of service, particularly the fact that service may be one of the critical factors in the customer's final purchase decision. Unfortunately, these same managers generally fail to recognize the *total* array of values which service provides in achieving customer satisfaction and in allowing the customer to make an effective trade-off (personally) between an extremely high level of quality and performance initially purchased and service to sustain the quality and performance over the life cycle.

Products Include or Generate Service Needs and Requirements

Embedded in every product, in one form or another, are service needs and requirements. Clearly, a mainframe computer needs to be maintained and repaired; therefore, it generates service requirements. It may not be so obvious that consumable products also require service. A good example is Coca-Cola syrup. The Coca-Cola Company sells syrup directly to hotels, restaurants, and other food service operators. The syrup is then mixed with ordinary water which is carbonated through a drink dispenser. The installation and servicing of that drink dispenser are critical elements in Coca-Cola's marketing of syrup to its customers. Another good example of embedded service involves McDonald's, which has developed a *standard approach* to the delivery service for food products (hamburgers, etc.) in its fast-food restaurants. In fact, all products, whether large capital equipment items like computers or consumable items like soft drinks or hamburgers, generate some type of service need.

An important step in developing a strategic service approach is to search for service needs and requirements embedded in or used in support of products. These services should then be isolated, defined and described, and managed and delivered strategically.

Product-Related Services

Products normally require delivery, installation, and maintenance and/or repair services. In some circumstances, products also have to be stored for later use.

In addition to these basic services, other product-related services include:

- Design and engineering and other professional services related to the application, installation, or use of the product
- Supply of consumables and other materials used by the product
- Refurbishment and replacement
- Upgrades, additions, and changes

These and other services are directly or indirectly required by the product user.

Managing the Product-Related Service Mix

Once these product-related services are identified, they must be packaged, described, and delivered. The decision as to whether these services should be provided independently, in parallel with the product, or as a subset of the product will depend on several issues, including the price elasticity of demand for these services and the cross elasticity of demand between the products and the services. I will discuss both of these issues in depth in Chap. 3. Under any circumstances, it is essential that the services be managed, controlled, and priced as a strategic package.

Service as a Perceived Requirement

I have already shown that a very important difference exists between the strategic management of tangible products and the management of both traditional services (banking, retail trade, etc.) and general after-sales services. This difference in service lies in the value and dimensions of *perception* as the major factor in the market. Since service is an intangible which is used only after purchase, the customer must make a purchase decision for service without really seeing it in advance of use.

Thus the customer's perception of services becomes critical in the decision to buy and use the specific services of a vendor.

Certainly, perceptions do exist in the product market. However, it is *critical to recognize* the very real difference which perception generates for the service business. A product is usually defined in marketing and merchandising terms through the combination of its form, fit, and function and its *label* or *perception* of quality or value. Very extensive market research suggests that the strength of the perceived value of the label in a product environment can generally create a price variation of 25 to 35 percent, or even as much as an order of magnitude (100 percent). This is true for IBM in the computer market, for DuPont in the chemical industry, for Eastman Kodak in the film market, and for companies in other product industries. However, for service it is extremely difficult not only to physically affix a label but also to advertise or merchandise the service form, fit, and function. It is, for example, very hard to physically depict the intangible service values in insurance, quick response and delivery in a retail store, on-time airline performance, automobile maintenance and repair services, etc.

Service Time—The Most Critical Factor in Service Perceptions

Market research suggests that the primary perceptions of services tend to be current views of the performance of the services at some future time. In essence, service form, fit, and function are primarily driven by a present view of what the future service performance will be, in terms of some dimension of time, such as:

- Waiting time to obtain service
- Reaction time to deliver service
- Length of time of the service

This market research suggests that it is *primarily* these perceptions of time and the specific *time dimensions* that are the most critical. Studies show that time perception is much more important than other factors such as service price, reputation, and quality. In summary, service perception is directly related to the user's view that *in the future* service will be provided *within the time parameters* and *time frame* required. This perceived service comfort level (i.e., the "warm and fuzzies") exists in almost all markets, including computers, restaurant service, banking services, health-care services, architectural services, and a very broad variety of other product or service industries.

Special Factors in the Critical Management of Time Perceptions in Service

The critical importance of the customer's perceptions of time cannot be overemphasized with regard to the concept of strategically marketed service. Time perception is much more sophisticated than the identification of a time factor. To demonstrate this, we can examine a specific service such as the cashing of checks in a bank. We can clearly see that there is a high level of perceived service if the potential customer, on entering the bank to cash a check, observes relatively short lines (of, say, 1 or 2 people rather than 5 or 6 or more). However, the lack of any waiting time or lines at all *does not necessarily lead to a better perception of service quality*. It might be easy to assume that since service time is the critical perceived value, it would be best to deliver service in the *least* possible time. However, time perception in service is much more complex.

While service satisfaction levels are determined *primarily* by service performance within the time frame required, once the *particular time threshold parameter* for a particular customer group is met, service satisfaction levels do not further improve. Typically, 80 percent of customers in most markets have a fairly *precise view* of the time dimension involved in their service requirements; they generally *do not* perceive more rapid delivery of service or higher levels of service once that performance time threshold is met.

If a group of customers is surveyed as to the level of satisfaction versus the service time requirement (as shown in Fig. 1-4), it will be clear that satisfaction levels increase rapidly as the time threshold is approached but do not increase further (and might even drop) after the threshold level is met. This critical "step" function (shown in Fig. 1-4) does exist.

It is quite clear that the customer can rarely measure or place value on too much service. In fact, *too much* service can lead to reduced customer satisfaction. Take the case of a customer entering a retail store. If no salesperson is available, or if there is a long waiting time, customer satisfaction is low. But if the salespeople become too aggressive or overly helpful, satisfaction may still be low.

In general, then, service is perceived largely when it is *absent within the time frame which the customer requires*. Too much service can be just as bad as too little service. Too little service creates customer dissatisfaction; too much service either is not perceived by the customer (and therefore is an extra cost which reduces profits) or is negatively viewed by the customer as service not required. This *unique nonlinear character* of service customer satisfaction, combined with time criticality, must

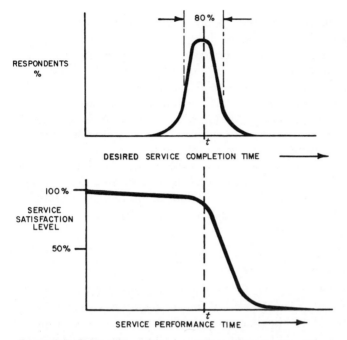

Figure 1-4. Relationship of desired service completion time to customer satisfaction levels.

be understood in managing service. My analysis suggests that with respect to services, a customer tends to make a very real trade-off between the price of a service and the quality of the service. This is achieved in terms of customer perceptions of the vendor's ability to meet, on a cost-effective basis, the customer's predefined service time dimensions for the service utilized.

Customer Dissatisfaction with Service Time

In this respect it is of interest to note that customers tend to be much less articulate if they have complaints about higher-priced services as compared with products. In effect, a customer tends to *complain* much more about products with regard to price. Market research shows that the resolved product complaints lead to future product brand loyalty. However, as service prices rise, there is a greater tendency for the customer to simply *walk away* from the service vendor rather than complain about the quality of service provided. Thus poor service satisfaction tends to generate significant losses in market share and control, particularly if it is broadly perceived.

Equally true is the fact that the customer's perceptions of service will vary as a function of perceptions of demand utilization. In effect, customers are less forgiving of lower service quality in situations of low demand; they are more willing to accept some reduction of service quality in high- or peak-demand situations. When waiting in line for service in a retail store, customers become very irritated if service time increases simply because clerks are answering phones or talking to each other. A customer is, however, willing to accept a delay if it is obvious that the salesclerk is working at a quick pace and the delay is due to the number of customers, or the work load. This, incidentally, may be a hidden cause of reduced customer satisfaction levels: service providers tend to "slack off" or reduce service quality in periods of low demand and overextend themselves in periods of high service demand.

Search for Time Factors in Service

It is most important, therefore, in developing strategic service to search for, identify, and measure the critical *time dimensions* as perceived by the customer. In effect, the starting point is to define the customer's market, isolate the key time dimensions of service, and determine the service requirements. It is critical that these time dimensions be measured as viewed through the eyes of the customer. Quite often the actual service performance time, as measured by the service deliverer, is *considerably different* from the perceived service performance time as measured by the service user.

This is also true in equipment maintenance and repair service, where the service organization tends to use the *elapsed time* between the customer's call for service and the initiation of the service response as a critical measure, whereas the customer tends to measure elapsed time from the initial failure of the equipment to the full repair of the equipment. This is particularly true in telephone service, where repair service time is typically measured from the receipt of a "trouble call," when there is a high focus on assigning a service technician to the problem. The customer tends to see the problem as starting when the phone is not in service; yet it might take a good deal of time for the customer to get to another phone to report the problem. Similarly, in a bank or retail store, the customer's waiting time starts when he or she enters and makes a decision to use the service or buy. The typical bank clerk or retail salesperson tends to see only the time at which the customer comes to the head of the queue as the start of the customer's waiting time.

Acceptable Time Values and Parameters

Even more important are the differences in dimensions between the vendor's view of acceptable service requirements and the consumer's view. The service vendor, for example, might be totally oriented toward providing service 8 hours a day, 5 days a week, because that is when the vendor's business operates. The service user, however, may require service on a 24-hour-a-day, 7-day-a-week basis. Obviously, the customer's perceptions are correct.

We have seen that customers cannot generally perceive higher levels of delivered service than they require. Thus creating a service portfolio geared to the requirements of a *specific* market segment or customer group can generate a significantly higher perception of service quality than delivering an average level of service to all segments. For example, for the *typical* men's clothing store, rapid tailoring service to adjust sizes may not be critical or profitable. But for the men's clothier focusing on big and tall sizes or upwardly mobile executives, it may be the critical strategic differentiator.

Approaches to Improving Service Perceptions

A number of strategies could be developed that can improve the perception of service quality and satisfaction levels. These include:

1. *Customizing standard services.* A number of services can be provided in a specific combination, or on a tailored basis, to meet the individual needs and requirements of a customer class or segment. American Express, for example, has developed a number of standard services in different packages to meet the needs of different customer groups.

2. *Controlling service quality and time standards.* The strict definition, articulation, and control of service can be accomplished through published standards, incentives, and training. McDonald's employs this approach in managing its fast-food service business.

3. *Creating tangible elements or functions of a service through increased focus on perceptions.* If a business can increase its focus on the service perceptions of potential or actual customers, it will be able to emphasize key service factors through merchandising, advertising, and promotion. In effect, a business can tell the customers that it understands, in their own terms, their specific service requirements. Domino Pizza's emphasis on its delivery service within 30 minutes is a good ex-

ample of how perception of time is utilized to market a service differentiation.

4. *Training employees in service issues.* Training employees to focus on customer sensitivity and service needs can result in a significant improvement in customers' perceptions in the field. SAS Airlines has found that intensive training of its flight attendants in service has created significant customer loyalty. Some firms use special compensation or bonuses, based on the measurement of levels of customer satisfaction, to increase employee awareness of the critical importance of service.

5. *Raising customer expectations of service levels and quality.* In defining service requirements, a business can change or adjust the levels of customer service to be offered. IBM standards for equipment service, for example, have become generally accepted in the industry. The innovation of "luxury" 24-hour, 7-day road service offered by automobile manufacturers such as Mercedes-Benz and the Cadillac Division of General Motors has been used to generate a significant strategic advantage for those automotive brands over normally available service levels.

Service Prices Should Be Based on Value in Use to the Customer

I have already pointed out that service quality is very strongly affected by customer perceptions of reality. A strategic approach to service can, therefore, provide an unusually high opportunity to employ value-in-use pricing, as opposed to cost plus markup, which is the typical mechanism used in product pricing.

Value in Use Defined

Value in use in a service environment is best thought of in terms of the cost to the customer in the absence of service. As an illustration, assume that you are traveling by car to a very important meeting at which you will complete a sales call that will result in a sales commission to you of $50,000. If your car fails to operate, you will, of course, try to get the car fixed by a mechanic from a nearby garage. In this case, the critical question is what price you are willing to pay for the service; equally important are what the garage mechanic should charge and what factors are influencing that price.

One approach to pricing the service is to examine the cost plus the normal markup for the mechanic's labor. Let's assume that the mechanic is paid $15 per hour; a normal markup of 100 percent makes the price $30 per hour; with a 30 percent profit margin, the final figure is $39 per hour. If 1 hour is needed for the service call, the call will be priced at approximately $40. Another approach is to relate the price to some percentage of the value of the automobile itself. The garage could, for example, arbitrarily charge a flat rate of 8 percent of the value of the automobile. If the car is a $30,000 Cadillac, the charge for service is $2400. If there are other garages in the area that are open and willing to provide service, you might look at a competitive price, which might be $40 for a service call. The final approach involves considering the loss incurred in the absence of the service—the loss of the $50,000 commission. In effect, this approach says charge some percentage of the loss to the customer: the *value in use* of service.

Thus we can see that there are several different approaches to pricing in a service market; some are directly affected by cost (the cost-plus-markup and competitive approaches), and others are not. In our example, if only one garage was open or willing to provide road service, or if you, the customer, were not aware of other competing garages, the last approach—service price based on *value in use*—would be the best from the *service provider's standpoint*. In addition, if a customer could find only one mechanic or garage available or did not know if other service providers were available, he or she would be willing to pay up to the value in use of service to obtain the repair service required. Thus pricing of service becomes strategically important particularly because of the options and opportunities for high-profit-margin pricing.

Price Elasticity of Demand in Service Pricing

Extensive market research has generally shown that the value-in-use pricing approach described above has great application in service markets, particularly because of two key factors:

1. The existence of a significant percentage of customers who are relatively insensitive to price with respect to service quality

2. The tendency to use service price as a surrogate for service quality

Market surveys typically show that 30 to 40 percent of all customers tend to be relatively *insensitive* to service prices, whereas only 10 to 15 percent tend to be *very sensitive* to price change. The average or typical customer (approximately 50 percent of the total universe) tends to equate price and quality. Market data strongly suggest that with respect to service, a higher percentage of the market is less sensitive (inelastic) with respect to price than is the case with product markets. I will discuss the specifics of service pricing in Chap. 7.

Use of Price as a Surrogate for Quality in Service

Because it is difficult to measure service quality, price is *often used as a surrogate for quality*. In this situation, an unusual relationship exists: *higher prices* lead to *higher demand*. This is particularly true for very time critical or demand critical services. For example, one typically looks for the highest-priced surgeon for open-heart surgery or the most expensive lawyer for defense in a murder case. In general, there is a very high correlation between time criticality and service price elasticity of demand. The more critical and tighter the time dimension, the higher the level of price insensitivity. In essence, the faster the service is needed or required, the more the customer is willing to pay for the service in order to guarantee the critical time level. Particularly because of the existence of a high degree of price *insensitivity* in services, the value-in-use approach to pricing can have significant benefits. Value-in-use prices can be significantly higher (on the order of 100 percent or more) than the cost-plus prices for the same services. The proactive* design of a services portfolio using specific time targets based on an evaluation of customers' *perceptions* and needs, as well as the application of value-in-use pricing for that portfolio, is a critical element in the strategic service concept.

The Need for Full Management and Control of Service

The major concepts of strategic service, as described above, suggest that there are substantial and very real differences between services and products. However, there is *one area* common to both services and tangible products: the need for full strategic-level management and control. In point of fact, service management requires greater discipline and focus to fully meet market requirements and needs for service. A critical, disciplined approach to the management, control, and allocation of people and parts, with specific emphasis on delivery on a time-critical basis, can generate significant values and profit margins in service.

---

*In this book, *proactive* means planned in advance on the basis of anticipated requirements for service, which are revealed by market research. A service organization that uses the less effective *reactive* approach reacts to individual customer needs as they occur.

The need for greater emphasis on the management of market perceptions and requirements in service does create a substantially more critical need for systems for management and control. In a product-manufacturing business, for example, the bulk of the data to be collected and organized in the control process relates to the *internal* manufacturing and distribution operations. In the service environment, it is also vitally important to make use of data about the *external market* in developing, implementing, and fully controlling service strategy.

Service quality and delivery can also be managed and controlled through a high focus on personnel, training and motivation, the establishment of specific service standards and objectives, and full emphasis on time discipline at all levels in the organization. In the service environment, the customer is closely linked to the marketing and sales operations of the service organization in a two-way relationship because the customer is often involved in the delivery of the service. Since sales, distribution, and the performance of service are so closely interrelated with customers' requirements and needs, it is difficult in service (as compared with product businesses) to *separate out* the marketing and distribution functions. Thus there is a critical need to manage these functions as well. In essence, quality in service requires a very high focus on *both* actual performance and marketing.

Management Approaches to Control or Reduce Service Costs

There are, of course, a number of management approaches that can be used to control or reduce service costs, given the recognition of critical time and perception factors discussed above.

Standardization. The establishment of standard, well-defined service modules or packages can lead to reduced costs through more efficient control of the human element in service delivery. With established standards, the services to be provided are clear to both the service delivery organization and the customer base.

Use of Alternative Customer-Based Delivery. This approach can reduce the personal involvement in service delivery and performance, or it can involve the customer in defining and delivering the service to meet specific needs. Customers can become more involved in service delivery if they are allowed to describe exact service requirements through a menu-based dialogue in the customer-service interface. In effect, service could be provided by means of a self-help package based on specific requirements that is delivered to the customer rather than a full-service package.

Specialized and Tailored Focus on Service Market Segments.
There are, of course, individual market segments which are sensitive
to different service requirements and levels of service quality and
time. Some customers want a maximum array of services and are willing to pay even a premium for it. Obviously, price-sensitive service
market segments also exist. In general, the more price-sensitive customers are willing to do more service themselves, including traveling
longer distances or performing some of the service distribution and
delivery functions which could be done by the service vendor. Ikea,
the retail furniture organization, is an example of a firm directed
specifically toward a customer base that prefers low prices. A customer will provide more of the service (delivery, installation, setup,
and assembly) to receive a lower price.

Use of Technology-Based Networks to Manage and Deliver Service.
Often services can be efficiently managed, delivered, and controlled by
computerized technology and network structures. Using a computerized network to more efficiently identify and assign resources to meet
service requirements and options, as well as to provide dynamic control,
can reduce overall service costs. The use of dynamically controlled hub
structures in airline and freight delivery service operations is an example of this approach.

**Establishment of Different Portfolios of Service Response and Com-
pletion Times.**   Service costs can be more effectively managed by
changing service response and delivery time characteristics to meet specific customer needs. In essence, some customers simply are willing to
wait longer than others. Others want accelerated service performance.

Management Approaches to Improve
Service Values

Besides being used to reduce costs, management strategies can be utilized to *improve service values and revenues*. There are a number of
methods for improving service values to the customer.

Combination of Standard Service Elements on a Customized Basis.
By creating a combination of standard service elements with a menu, it
is possible to produce a customized service package that the customer
perceives as being of higher quality. With this approach a service organization can emphasize high-value-in-use services, priced at a high level,
for the inelastic customer segments and lower-priced service portfolios
for the price-sensitive segments.

Proactive Identification of High-Value-in-Use Service Requirements by Specific Customer Segments. This method can also be used to maximize profit margins. By processing information from customer service activities, a service vendor can pinpoint new opportunities for profitable service.

Management of Service Delivery and Demand. A combination of pricing and scheduling can be used to shift customer demands over time. In effect, setting higher prices for service provided in peak-demand periods can cause some customers to change their demand requirement. The other customers who are willing to pay for critical service in peak demand can be scheduled on the basis of the additional service delivery capabilities they are willing to pay for. Technology and the use of temporary, part-time, or subcontract employees can also be used to shift the capability to meet changing demand requirements.

Enforcement of Strict Quality-Control Standards. A most important way to retain or improve perceived value to the customer is to increase the comfort level—that is, assure the customer that service will be performed in accordance with strict standards. In essence, the comfort level of the customer can be improved through the management of the interface between the customer and the service employee. Service personnel's commitment to this level of performance can be achieved through a focus on established service standards and training.

Use of Contracts versus Time-and-Materials Pricing. Many services are provided on a time-and-materials basis. Establishing a fixed price for a service improves the customer's confidence that the service required will be provided within a budget. The service vendor can add a surcharge or premium for the reduced risk to the customer of a budget overrun. Wherever possible, service organizations should attempt to provide a high percentage of their activity on a contract basis. While the time-and-materials approach appears to offer the highest profit and least risk in the short run, it reduces the ability to plan and schedule service resources. Contracts are easier to manage and control, since the customer's commitment to the service is made over a period of time on a fixed-price basis rather than on a per-incident basis.

Efforts to Increase Customer Involvement. A service organization can focus on customer involvement to increase value if it is *justifiable* in terms of the customer's value in use or perception of service quality improvement. This is particularly true, since pragmatic experience of the typical customer generally suggests that increased customer involvement should result in price reduction.

Management Approaches to Improve
Service Productivity

Finally, it is important to recognize that service productivity and efficiency can be improved or changed in response to changing requirements and needs and through the use of new technology for control, coordination, and communications.

From the management standpoint, service creates significant problems which are not found in a manufacturing environment. Since a service organization cannot inventory and stock services, and since the production and consumption of service must usually occur simultaneously, it is necessary to make efficient use of full capacity and capability to perform. Service management and delivery systems and technology can be used to efficiently adjust service supply to meet demand. For example, computerized technology and systems can be employed to significantly improve the ability to handle calls for assistance and service; service capabilities can be optimally allocated and dispatched in response to the different needs and requirements of the customer base. The critical time discipline required in service means that people, parts, and materials must be efficiently tracked, controlled, and assigned. Of even greater importance is the need to collect accurate data concerning the changing service requirements and needs of customers. The results of previous service dispatch and allocations can be used to develop market knowledge which can become the basis for the planned development of the future service portfolio and value-in-use service pricing.

It is critically important in strategically managing a service operation to recognize that the client participates directly in the delivery and use of service. Thus the personnel who deliver service are the key to quality, and strict quality standards, training, and incentives are more critical in service than they are in tangible-product businesses.

In summary, strategic service represents a very significant opportunity for the generation of revenues and profits. Attention to the key values of service, the importance of market perception, and the use of management systems and technology can lead to maximization of this opportunity.

Whether one is operating a service business per se or providing service in the context of a product business, improving customers' perceptions of service as well as actual service performance with respect to time and other factors can lead to increased market satisfaction and share and higher revenues, but potentially at an increasing operational cost. Thus the most profitable service strategy is one which is fine-tuned to the specific service requirements of the targeted market, with a particular focus on time sensitivity. The best market opportunities can be found by identifying a high-density base of customers with a high value in use or time criticality. I will discuss this approach in more detail in Chaps. 7, 8, and 9.

A Global, Integrated Viewpoint

In developing a strategic service approach, it is important to have a global view of service market requirements in terms of market structure, specific market segments, and service portfolio needs. The service operating strategy must include both a delivery approach and the marketing concept. These, in turn, should drive the actual service delivery and the marketing, sales, and pricing functions. The overall process is continually controlled by examining both the changing and emerging market requirements and needs and the existing strategies and competition to see if new strategies should be developed or current ones revised. Service strategies can be developed on the basis of perceived levels of service requirements and the cost of service delivery. This involves a portfolio of services which are either standard or highly differentiated and which vary in cost, depending on the different target markets: price-sensitive, linear, and price-insensitive.

The use of a strategic service concept has created significant changes in the way service in general and field service in particular are managed, operated, organized, and controlled. The general trend over the last 10 to 15 years, as well as projections, shows a transition in the way service is operated: as a decentralized cost center, then as a profit center, and ultimately as a centralized, strategic line of business. There is also a growing use of management systems and technology. The effective use of market and operational data to optimize the delivery of service to specific market segments depends on the increasing use of integrated management systems, field data collection systems, and artificial intelligence and diagnostics for the management, direction, and control of service.

Practical Steps in Applying the Strategic Service Concept

In order to develop the concept of strategic service, you need to think about your business in terms of the key ideas outlined above and follow the process shown in Fig. 1-5. For a business involving a tangible product, such as a manufacturing firm, the first step is to look for the service components: identify the service requirements of the product in terms of customer needs and requirements. For a service business such as a bank or an insurance company, which does not involve tangible prod-

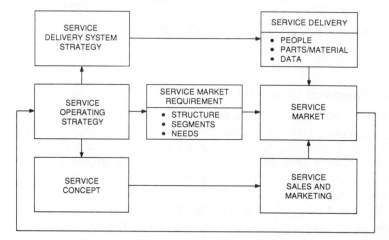

Figure 1-5. The strategic service process.

ucts, the first step is to identify the key requirements for service in the customer's terms. For both types of businesses (product and service), it is necessary to estimate the amount spent by the customer on these key services over the life cycle of use so that market potential and opportunity can be determined. This analysis is then used to develop the service operating strategy. The strategy is articulated in terms of the overall service concept and service delivery system.

At this stage the services can be packaged and described in a form which can be marketed to the particular customer segment. We must recognize that different customer segments want and are willing to pay for different portfolios of service. It is necessary to establish a preliminary price for each package of services and decide how the package will be offered and delivered to the customer. Specifically, should the services be offered separately, as part of the general bundle of product and services, or as part of an overall service mix? The service staffing and resources plan must then be developed to deliver the service portfolio defined by the market requirements and needs.

Once this is done, we need to look at the staffing and support costs of delivering the services and determine how to manage and control these service costs, as well as improve productivity. We must then develop the final marketing and sales approach and pricing. The final step involves the development of a service management strategy to coordinate service and direct the strategic service delivery process. Each of these steps is discussed in more detail in the chapters that follow.

2

Identifying Present and Emerging Market Opportunities for Service and Support

The General Market for Service and Support

The market demand for service and support has become increasingly important as the economy has matured. In essence, while the portion of the gross national product (GNP) associated with the manufacture of goods has been slowly and erratically growing, the overall service industry has become very significant. Our economy now produces much more "services" than "goods," and this ratio is continuously increasing.

In addition to the traditional services such as banking and finance, health care, retail trade, and transportation and distribution, there are services provided by goods producers. The maintenance and support of plant and equipment used in producing the goods and field and customer services extended by product manufacturers, distributors, and independent service providers to end users are additional services which must also be considered.

These embedded services, added to the "stand-alone" service busi-

nesses and activities, have turned the United States (and most other developed nations) into a predominantly service-oriented economy. Unfortunately, the development of knowledge of the structure of the
service market has not kept pace with the growth of this market. Relatively little detailed information is available on the service industry in
the United States, since much of the economic and industrial structure
information is developed on the basis of, and oriented to, manufactured
goods.

Traditional Service Organizations Supplying Market Needs

There are a great number of organizations operating in the economy
which produce a service rather than a tangible good. These organizations supply the traditional services, including:

Transportation and distribution

Communications

Wholesale and retail trade

Finance, insurance, and real estate

Business and professional services

Government services

Customer service can also be found in all types of organizations, including those involved in the manufacture of tangible products. In this
analysis, however, we are primarily concerned with organizations which
offer *both* customer and field service and thus provide a framework for
dealing with service on an integrated basis. This is not to suggest that
the concept of strategic service is not broadly applicable; nevertheless,
the payoff and value are highest in situations in which service is provided globally.

Product-Based Service Organizations

Of all the service businesses in the United States, the field service organizations have experienced *substantial growth*. These organizations are
concerned with the design, installation, maintenance, and repair of
field- and plant-based products, equipment, and systems, particularly
high technology. Service and support are provided for many types and
classes of products, including data processing and office automation
equipment, office products (copying equipment, typewriters, etc.), tele-

communications equipment, medical electronics equipment, process control and plant automation equipment, and heating, ventilation, and air-conditioning equipment. This particular segment of the total service market is growing at a more rapid rate than the traditional services sector.

Types of Product-Based Service Organizations

Four types of product-based service organizations provide and deliver service and support.

1. *Manufacturer-owned and -operated service organizations.* These include the service arms of manufacturers of products, equipment, and systems. They provide customer service and support and installation, maintenance, and repair services on a local, regional, or national basis.

2. *Dealer, distributor, and retailer service organizations.* These provide service forces to support the sale and distribution of products and/or services.

3. *Independent (third-party) and contractor service organizations.* These include local, regional, and national service organizations that provide some mix of service and support but do not sell or distribute products and equipment per se.

4. *User-owned internal service forces.* These are service organizations owned and operated by user firms and corporations which manage and control service and support for their own (internal) plant, equipment, and systems. They may provide the services through an in-house service force, on a contract basis, or through a combination of internal and external staff.

Almost no published data are available on the size and structure of the product service industry in the United States. Our best information suggests that there are about 250,000 service organizations, of which approximately 80,000 are of reasonable size (i.e., with five or more service personnel).

The biggest of these service organizations are involved in servicing and supporting information systems, office products, and telecommunications equipment; these are generally the organizations which have moved most aggressively toward the use of sophisticated management and marketing approaches in running services as full lines of business. However, there are fairly large service forces in other organizations which are also undergoing significant expansion. For example, radio,

TV, and appliance distributors—such as Sears, Montgomery Ward, and a number of regional retail organizations—are currently expanding their service operations. The plant maintenance service departments of major manufacturers constitute the largest number of user-oriented and -owned service forces and are generally found in the chemical industry, the pulp and paper industry, the petrochemical and oil industries, and utilities. Obviously, there are also a very large number of smaller service organizations for the aftermarket support of automobiles, marine vessels, and other vehicles.

Overall Service Market Structure

An economic evaluation of the service market shows that for service as a line of business, the cost of operations as a percentage of sales is one of the lowest, and gross profits, therefore, are among the highest. Service also produces the highest return on equity and return on assets. Executive compensation in the service industry is typically the highest.

Historically, services were generally provided through a large number of small enterprises because of the ease of entry, the lack of recognition of economies of scale, and the fragmented nature of the market. These factors are all changing because of:

Increasing customer requirements and needs for services and the associated willingness to pay

Increased availability of technology and systems to manage service delivery

A new strategic focus on service as a business opportunity

Mergers and acquisitions involving smaller service organizations to form larger, integrated service capabilities

Of these new trends, one of the most significant is the provision of full service and support for products and equipment in the field. This growth is being created by several key pressures, including:

Increased installed base of products and technology

Blurring of technological distinctions between products, placing greater emphasis on service as the key differentiator

Increased dependence on products and technology for day-to-day operations, creating increased service value in use

Under any test, the service industry is quite attractive. Currently available data show that in general, the service industry—consisting of business services, third-party maintenance and repair services, and other miscellaneous services—has the highest growth rate and generates the highest return on assets and return on net worth when compared with any other sector. While this is not a comprehensive portrayal, it does give some insight into the high growth opportunity which service offers as a strategic line of business.

The Economic Structure of the Service Market

It is quite clear that the field service and support organizations generate substantial economic value in today's economy. Unfortunately, much of our production of goods and services is tied to industrial classifications and structures which are biased toward tangible products. Thus it is quite often difficult to isolate the service component of product support in the gross national product. In those segments of the economy which are purely service-oriented, such as banking and retail trade, standard economic and government reporting can be utilized. However, the equipment and plant *service* components embedded in such segments as manufacturing, utilities, and transportation are much more difficult to isolate. In addition, even internal accounting and financial reporting do not provide a full picture of the full services provided by industrial firms.

Using both Department of Commerce data and my own research, I have attempted to estimate the size of the general service expenditures within the context of the gross national product, using the Standard Industrial Code structure. I have tried to give special attention to the size of the equipment field service business base within this context in the manufacturing industry.

As indicated in Table 2-1, this analysis shows that the total service market is very substantial when one considers the broad range of service provided in our fully developed economy, by major industrial segment. My estimate of the total size of the service market, which includes the equipment-related services embedded, to a large extent, in the manufacturing sector, suggests that the equipment field service industry is quite substantial.

My analysis indicates that in 1988 the manufacturing-oriented field service segment represented a $128 billion market. Equipment services in communications, utilities, and government increased this figure to

Table 2-1. Gross National Product, 1988, by Industry and Major Product
Type (In $ Billions)

| Industry | Major product type | | Total |
	Goods*	Service†	
Agriculture, forestry, fisheries	81.2	19.6	100.8
Mining	62.7	28.0	90.7
Construction	81.9	150.1	232.0
Manufacturing	778.7	127.7	906.4
Transportation	33.4	126.7	160.1
Communications	25.4	103.1	128.5
Utilities	60.1	84.7	144.8
Wholesale	70.0	262.4	332.4
Retail	92.8	361.1	453.9
Finance, insurance, real estate	426.9	396.5	823.4
Services	—	842.6	842.6
Government	95.7	472.7	568.4
Other	12.8	18.5	31.3
Total	1813.2	2993.7	4806.9

*Includes structures production.
†Includes $547 billion for product service normally embedded in goods production and
delivery.
SOURCE: U.S. Department of Commerce and D. F. Blumberg & Associates research.

$547 billion. The total value of services in the U.S. economy was almost
$3 trillion out of a total GNP of $4.8 trillion. I estimate that the equipment service market will continue to grow at a rate of more than 17 percent into the 1990s (see Table 2-2). In summary, service is now more
than 60 percent of the total economy, and equipment service is one of
the rapidly growing areas in the total service market.

The existence of this large service market business opportunity is now
recognized. Over the last 10 years many firms have established separate
service divisions or profit centers which focus on specific service opportunities and needs of their customer base. Senior industry executives
will increasingly recognize the growing contribution of service, as a line
of business, to both corporate revenues and corporate profits. Several
firms are expanding into new services such as systems integration and
total site services.

Table 2-2. Products versus Service in the U.S. Economy (In $ Billions)

Gross national product element	1986	1987	Year 1988 (est.)	1989 (est.)	1990 (est.)	Compound annual growth rate (CAGR), %
Goods production	1697.9	1792.5	1912.7	2060.0	2239.2	7.1
Service embedded in goods production and delivery	392.2	467.8	547.0	640.7	752.4	17.7
Service provided separately	2118.4	2295.7	2446.7	2576.8	2742.4	6.7
Structures production	424.0	438.4	447.5	457.7	470.5	2.6
Total GNP	4240.3	4526.7	4806.9	5114.5	5452.1	6.5
Service component of GNP	2510.6	2763.5	2993.7	3237.5	3494.8	8.6
Ratio of service to total GNP	59.2%	61.0%	62.3%	63.3%	64.1%	

SOURCE: GNP data—U.S. Bureau of Economic Analysis and Bureau of Labor Statistics; service data—D. F. Blumberg & Associates proprietary studies.

Independent, or Third-Party, Service as a Business Opportunity

The importance of service and support to the customer continues to increase substantially over time—in general as well as in high-tech markets. For the customer, the quality of service has become increasingly critical in the process of choosing between vendors considered as a first choice and those who are not acceptable or who would be considered only because of a very significant price discount. Whether dealing with a retail store, a restaurant, a professional such as a doctor or lawyer, or a bank, customers want to know that the vendor can provide services which:

- Meet their service time and service response requirements in a cost-effective manner
- Constitute the particular portfolio they require
- Are sensitive to their changing requirements and needs

In high-tech markets in particular, the accelerating technological advancements, increasing dependence on technological support for day-to-day business activities, and the sophisticated work being done with the technology all serve to increase the emphasis on service and support. As customers tend to rely more heavily on the installed base of technology, including the complex software and operating procedures, they want a service provider who understands the operating environment and can deliver the necessary services to keep the technology running in the event of a problem or failure.

However, service needs and requirements do differ significantly from one user group to another. Most vendors are not sensitive to these differences in service needs and requirements or to different economies associated with service delivery alternatives or willingness to pay. Thus major new growth areas are emerging in the high-tech markets for those vendors who can recognize, package, and deliver the proper set of services for each customer base.

A good growth area in the high-tech markets is the provision of service *as a separate line of business* for design, engineering, installation, and maintenance and repair. In the past, these types of services were provided by the original equipment manufacturer (OEM) or by a manufacturer's distributor (the "first party") for the user (the "second party"). However, over the last 10 years, a new class of service organizations has emerged: the "third-party" maintainers. These organizations have been making installation, maintenance, and repair services (and, recently, design and engineering services) available to the end users, either with the authorization and support of the OEM or directly. The advantage to the end users is that the independent, or third-party, service organizations can provide full service to meet their needs and requirements.

Factors Influencing Service Growth in the High-Tech Markets

A number of factors are influencing the rapid growth of third-party service in the high-tech markets. A primary factor is increased customer emphasis on service response and quality because of the users' growing dependence on a full array of technology for day-to-day business operations. Another factor is the proliferation of technology from new firms that are entering the marketplace without service capabilities. These new firms produce personal computers, advanced work stations, local area networks, and peripheral equipment such as printers, storage units, and monitors. They are often reluctant to provide full service because of their lack of installed-base density or the need to rapidly build up a service force capable of handling the complex, technologically intensive nature of service. Developing a full-service capability also often necessitates major capital expenditures on parts and the establishment of a nationwide logistics system and infrastructure, which the smaller firms wish to avoid.

The larger service forces which are in place have already achieved some economies of scale through the establishment of computerized call management and logistics support systems, the establishment of depot and repair facilities, and the existence of a trained labor force. The small, new manufacturers and other small, mature, slow-growth firms have not developed an installed base that is sufficient to achieve these economies of scale. However, customers' concerns for service credibility and capability require that all firms they deal with provide service when and where required, particularly on-site. For most industrial or business user firms, carry-in or mail-in service at a central depot is not sufficient. Thus for both types of manufacturers (the new firms and the small, mature organizations), the third-party service organizations are an attractive alternative for providing service to customers. The third-party organizations can offer nationwide service or coverage in those areas in which the manufacturer or systems integrator has not developed a base that is dense enough to support a service organization. The small manufacturers do not incur the expense associated with maintaining a full-service structure.

A third factor influencing the growth of the independent service organizations is the deregulation of the telecommunications industry. With this deregulation, service, which was originally included in the monthly rental fee for the telecommunications equipment, was required to become a separate cost and user-expense item. Recent studies of decision makers in telecommunications service have shown an increased interest in using independent service providers, particularly service vendors offering integrated, single-point-of-contact network support.

Another major factor influencing the growing demand for third-party service is an increasing interest in service cost containment. Users of service are no longer satisfied in being able to buy service from the original equipment manufacturer or a distributor *only*; they are looking for true alternatives. Service users want improved service response and quality. They also want to reduce service problems and control service costs, including the costs of downtime.

The Single Service Manager Concept

Generally, the managers of the service users deal with a minimum of five or more service vendors at one location, such as a large office or plant site. Therefore, the possible use of a single *integrated* service manager (i.e., a service organization which can manage a significant percentage of, if not all, service requirements) is also of interest to service users. This growing interest in an *integrated, single-source* service manager is due to users' needs:

1. To reduce *total service costs* and charges from all service vendors, including downtime costs (the costs incurred in the event that services are not provided). In fact, in market surveys users express a willingness to pay up to a 10 percent premium over current market prices for service from an integrated, single-source service supplier.

2. To avoid *finger pointing*. Users need rapid and accurate identification of problems involving service vendors. (Who is responsible for what service?)

3. To improve *overall service responsiveness and quality*.

4. To reduce the *time and effort* required to find the correct service provider and report the service needed.

Interest in this integrated, or single-point-of-contact, service will continue to grow among businesses that produce high-tech products, particularly as the products become more interactive and interlinked.

Examples of the Single Service Manager Concept in Independent, or Third-Party, Service

The concept of providing full service—either as an activity independent of product or technology sales (i.e., third-party maintenance) or as a strategic line of business (i.e., embedding tangible products into the total service portfolio)—is widely applicable. A number of firms in high-tech markets—including data processing, office automation, and telecommunications—have recognized this opportunity and now offer a full array of services which go beyond the product technology to meet their customers' needs and requirements. IBM, in the data processing industry, now provides a full range of services, including:

- Systems design and engineering
- Installation
- Network service and support
- Hardware repair
- Software service
- Service management (including acting as a single point of contact to supervise other service providers)

These services are provided independently to IBM customers, regardless of the IBM hardware or product technology involved. Control Data, as another example, generates a reasonable volume of business providing third-party maintenance and repair services for DEC and IBM products. DEC provides services for non-DEC technology, particularly where it is networked with DEC equipment; in other words, DEC provides total "seamless" service for its customer base.

Examples of full, independent service can also be found in a wide variety of other industries. Sears, for example, in the retail industry, offers its customers a broad array of financial, home improvement, and product repair services. Many major banks, such as Citibank, stress their comprehensive portfolio of services (checking and savings accounts, loans, investment advice, etc.), designed to meet the requirements of their various customer segments.

The concept of a full-service provider can be extended to include *all* the service requirements of a customer at a particular location. By examining the total service need, driven by the characteristics of the site, and the customer base, additional service requirements may be identified. Service Master, for example, has used this approach; it offers industrial, commercial, and residential customers a full portfolio of services for the maintenance and repair of the site and building. Other site-oriented services—such as full lawn and garden care, pool services, and building equipment service (for elevators, heating, ventilation, etc.)—can be extended to provide a total site-oriented portfolio of services.

Independent services could be provided in any number of situations. A menswear retailer can provide full service that includes custom tailoring; help in selecting and coordinating suits, ties, shirts, and accessories; and refitting in the event of a weight change. Boyd's, a very successful men's clothing store in Philadelphia, provides a full package of services, including valet parking, the serving of wine and soft drinks, and help in picking out matching ties, shirts, and accessories. This total service commitment to the targeted male buyers is enhanced through the creation of separate style and size departments (European styles, big and tall men, etc.). The critical key, however, is the concept of a single-service salesperson who handles a customer from the moment he enters the store to the time he leaves. The various services are orchestrated and provided through this one salesperson, who will also deal with the customer on subsequent visits.

The concept of total, independent service is also being used by major automobile manufacturers. Both Mercedes and the Cadillac Division of General Motors now provide a total service commitment for their car lines. This includes delivery, preventive maintenance, and on-the-road repair service, available through a call to an 800 number. This particular portfolio of services has been tailored for the luxury-automobile buyers and is offered as an independent service package for the product buyer and user.

The key factors in this independent-service strategy are providing an array of services to meet specific customer needs and requirements, delivering service within the time frame required, and making the services available as part of the full product or technology offering (bundled) or as a separate package (unbundled). By isolating the various service needs and requirements, it is possible to deal with service in its total or strategic framework.

How Independent Service Offerings
Pull Through Products or
Technology

We can easily see how service requirements are "pulled through" by the sale of a product or technology. What is less recognized is that the reverse is also true; the sale of an independent service portfolio can "pull through" product or technology requirements. I have described this phenomenon of cross elasticity of demand earlier, but it deserves repeating at this point in the discussion. Satisfied users of service will often turn to the service vendor for advice on, and the sale of, products or technology. A satisfied service customer feels very comfortable in dealing with the same vendor for future products and technology as well as service; the customer knows that the quality of service already received will continue. Thus in addition to directly generating revenue and profit, a full-service portfolio can also produce a demand for additional product sales.

Identifying and Developing the Independent-Service Strategy

Historically, service organizations in general and those in high-tech markets have been developed from a product-oriented perspective. The vendor typically examined the service requirements and needs of a product and established the service portfolio on the basis of the services the customer required to support the product. In this approach, service was viewed as support to the *product* sale, not as a full requirement in itself.

While this approach might work in the introductory stage of a product's life cycle, where the new product tends to define its own service needs, it is neither applicable nor efficient in general. In today's markets, the service needs and requirements of a particular technology or product will vary dramatically as a function of the user segment, application, degree of integration, and—of greatest importance—degree of technological interdependence. To the extent that the user is highly dependent upon equipment or technology for day-to-day, hour-by-hour, minute-by-minute, and even second-by-second operations, the value in use of the equipment or technology can become quite high. Since service requirements are determined to a large extent by equipment criticality, one might find that the same product has different values in use and different service response and repair time requirements simply because of differences in customer use, independent of the product technology.

Vertical Market Segmentation

In analyzing and evaluating the changing and emerging structures of the service market and competition, it is increasingly clear that a service segmentation approach based upon factors other than a focus on products can best determine the service portfolio for a given service vendor. One of the best approaches is to focus on the service requirements of vertical, or user-oriented, market segments. These vertical market segments, broadly defined by Standard Industrial Codes (SICs), include banking and health care. An examination of unique or specialized service requirements of vertical market segments can be used to determine specific service portfolios which have a high value in use for those segments. For example, high-tech manufacturers, doctors, and men's clothing retailers are specific vertical segments in the industrial and commercial markets. Homeowners, senior citizens, and high-income families with children are examples of consumer segments.

The general structure of vertical market segments can be described as follows:

1. *In general, each segment can be clearly identified and defined.* The industrial and commercial segments are usually represented by one or more trade or professional associations and are served by those associations, as well as by magazines and other professional groups. The individual industrial market segments are also usually served by one or more trade shows. In the consumer markets, there are various targeted magazines and other media. The elements of each of the market segments—including small, medium, and large organizations and their support vendors—can also be clearly identified, through available government data sources such as Department of Commerce reports.

2. *A reasonably high degree of standardization exists for technology and density in firms of the same size within a segment.* This is generally a result of vendors typically focusing on vertical segments as a way of identifying market niches and requirements.

3. *Users in a segment may be highly dependent upon products and technology for day-to-day, minute-by-minute operations.* Thus the value in use of service could be quite high.

4. *Vertical segments may not be currently the focus of an orderly or rational marketing approach by the existing service vendors.* When the service vendors are present within the segments, they are typically oriented toward specific *product* service, and their existence within the vertical segments is random.

5. *The expenditures for services within each segment can be quite high and are usually growing rapidly.*

An in-depth understanding of the service needs of individual vertical market segments can be the basis for an optimum service portfolio and market penetration strategy for existing service organizations and for those new organizations attempting to enter the service market. The specific needs will also vary by the size of each firm within a vertical market segment; therefore, segmentation can be more detailed.

The information technology market is the most attractive of the vertical market segments because of a high degree of installed-base density, a well-defined market structure, easy access to decision makers, and a high value in use for service. Included in this segment are banks, insurance companies, transportation and distribution organizations, hospitals, retail stores, and high-tech manufacturers. The independent-service opportunities will, of course, differ by the types of offerings within this segment.

Individual vertical market segments can be quite attractive in terms of both opportunity and market size, and a number of the product-oriented service organizations do actively participate in these vertical market segments at present. However, their *lack of focus* on the service needs of different vertical market segments is an important reason why they have failed to achieve a higher level of growth and profitability. By developing a full-service strategy and a full-service portfolio—that is, by focusing on the present and emerging needs and requirements of specific *vertical market segments*—organizations can improve revenue growth and profitability. Each vertical market segment requires specific attention so that dynamic strategies can be developed for successfully penetrating the most attractive market niches, where both service demand and value in use are high. Since individual market segments differ greatly in terms of general structure, characterization, equipment density, and service market potential, unique selling propositions can be developed which will prevail over the approaches of the product-oriented service vendors.

Other Market Segmentation Approaches

Vertical market segmentation, based on SIC definitions, is not the only way to identify service market opportunities and requirements. Other segmentation approaches can be used.

Location.   Customers in different parts of the country or different areas of the world have different service requirements and needs. Also, customers that operate in several locations have different service requirements than customers at a single location.

Customer Density or Proximity.   Customers located near other, similar customers have different service requirements and needs than customers that are widely separated. This is due in part to expectations, as well as to standard practice. A customer based in downtown Manhattan, for example, will want and expect a different level of service (in terms of response and repair time, time-of-day and day-of-week coverage, etc.) than a customer based in an isolated farm community in Nebraska.

Service Quality Level and Willingness to Pay.   A third segmentation approach is based on differences in customers' demands for service quality and their willingness to pay. As with products, some customers demand and are willing to pay for high-quality, highly responsive service; at the other end of the spectrum are customers that want little or no service or prefer self-maintenance, generally out of a much lower desire to pay for service. The required service portfolio will be very different for those different segments.

Steps in Developing a Service Strategy Based on Market Segmentation

In general, a successful independent-service strategy can be developed as follows:

1. *Identify and define the user group(s) to be served* on the basis of structural characteristics (vertical market segmentation) and industrial classifications (e.g., banks, hospitals, manufacturing firms, and consumers), location, customer density or proximity, and service quality required and willingness to pay.

2. *Determine the service requirements and needs of these market segments,* both in general and with respect to products and technology.

3. *Establish a service portfolio which meets these requirements and needs.* Service should be provided in a cost-effective manner, on the basis of the density of customers to be served and the product and technology knowledge and service capability of the vendor.

4. *Deliver the service portfolio independently* or together with the product or technology. It is important that the vendor explicitly define the service portfolio as an item that is separate from the product or technology. The vendor should offer both and provide the tangible product or technology in one of the following three ways:
   - Separately
   - Linked to the service portfolio through a discount or some other merchandising scheme
   - As a subset of the service portfolio

The key step is market segmentation. This leads to the explicit definition of service in terms of the customer's requirements, rather than the product framework, and the development and delivery of the tailored service portfolio. Packaging the service portfolio independently or together with the product or technology offered, if it exists, enables the customer to make the best choice. The customer could be encouraged to purchase *both* the product and the service portfolio through packaging, pricing, and other merchandising methods. More important, however, is giving the customer a clear choice.

If the service portfolio has been well defined, is delivered on a cost-effective basis, and is priced properly (see Chap. 7), the customer will purchase it. In addition, the purchase of the service portfolio will either initially or ultimately lead to the purchase of more services and products or technology (if offered). The steps described above should be followed to develop, package, and deliver services that meet customer requirements and needs, and vendors should be fully committed to meeting those requirements and needs.

Ways to Enter the Independent-Service Market

There are three basic approaches that organizations can take to competitively enter and participate in the emerging service marketplace. The first involves offering a service contract or portfolio directly to the end user for services required but not available elsewhere, or provided uniquely by only one organization for a high price. For example, in the high-tech markets (which have traditionally been a focus of new direct-service offerings) are obsolete product lines or equipment not serviced directly by the manufacturer. Independent service organizations have taken advantage of such situations. They establish a portfolio in a market where they are not in direct competition* with the service organization of the manufacturer or distributor (the first party). Once established as an acceptable service vendor, the independent service organization can extend the initial agreement with the end user to provide full service for the array of needs at the customer site. This approach can also be developed by focusing on other nonhardware or nontechnology services that are required but not available from the manufacturer or distributor.

A second approach is to focus directly on the end-user market, with emphasis on the specific service needs of key vertical segments. This is

*Arguments for manufacturer support of independent service organizations in direct competition are discussed in App. A.

particularly useful with respect to the provision of network services or full site services. In essence, the second approach is to provide full services on an integrated, managed basis for a specific user or customer environment. This approach requires developing knowledge of a *specific* service environment and then using that specialization to gain market entry.

A third strategy which has been used by some service organizations to enter the market is to establish an "authorized service agreement" with another firm which initiates the product, technology, or service sale. For example, a service agreement may be established with a small, new high-tech manufacturer or a smaller, mature firm which does not have a service force in place on a national or regional basis. The agreement may also be with a high-tech manufacturer whose primary concern is selling products and equipment rather than providing service and support. The servicing of the high-tech equipment is generally done under the independent service organization's name, and the service organization is responsible for billing the end user. The high-tech manufacturers are thus able to provide their end users with full service and support without making an investment in service management systems and technology, labor forces, or parts. In an alternative approach, a service organization offers its services to the manufacturer on an hourly basis and bills the manufacturer directly for labor. The manufacturer, in this case, is responsible for billing the final customer for the services rendered. In essence, the service organization is "subcontracted" by the manufacturer or distributor to the user to provide a full range of service and support.

Distributor Service and Support

In many markets, the *independent distributor* plays a key role, not only in the sale of products and equipment but also in the provision of services. Distributors are generally strongest in local and regional servicing. The independent distributor will provide a full range of services, including delivery, installation, warranty, support, training, and maintenance. In some cases, a high-tech-equipment manufacturer may use local distributors for the sale and maintenance of certain product lines, while for other specific products, the manufacturer may establish, in addition to the distributor service and support, an authorized service agreement with a national (third-party) organization. Thus the third market penetration strategy described above (operating under an agreement) could be employed with a distributor. A service organization could also *become* a direct distributor to either enter the service market or augment or extend its service portfolio.

To review, there are three broad market penetration strategies:

- Providing service directly to users, with a focus on services not currently available

- Providing service directly to end users on the basis of a knowledge of vertical market segments, including their specific requirements

- Providing service directly to end users under authorized service agreements or indirectly through manufacturers or distributors, or becoming a distributor to provide service directly

Where there is no product or technology involved, market penetration can be achieved in one of two ways:

- *Directly*, by focusing on the service needs and requirements of specific market segments and/or niches

- *Indirectly*, through other service or product organizations in a formal or partner relationship

I will discuss strategic service partnering below.

Strategic Service Partnering Opportunities

The continuing increase in the growth of user demand for integrated, single-source service, coupled with the desire of service organizations to identify and expand into new market niches and erect competitive barriers, has created increasing interest in the concept of strategic service partnering. Limited partnering or joint-venture relationships have existed for some time in the service industry. For example, it is not unusual for a small manufacturer without extensive service capability, or an offshore company contemplating entry into the U.S. market, to consider entering into some type of agreement with an existing nationwide service organization to provide general service for its customer base. In the case where the manufacturer enters into a partnership agreement with a service organization, the service organization agrees to provide regional or nationwide service, and the manufacturer agrees to provide the service organization with parts, diagnostics, and, in some cases, training for the service organization's customer engineer and backup depot repair.

This simple partnering relationship provides advantages for both participants. The service organization gains additional service revenues by providing service directly to the users of the manufacturer's products without having to invest in parts, diagnostics, and support. The manufacturing organization, on the other hand, gains the advantage of an already existing service organization without having to invest in the creation of a service force or divert management attention away from the primary mission of product manufacturing and distribution. In the area of third-party maintenance for computers, for example, TRW has made use of such partnering agreements in the early stages of development of its independent-service business. In fact, this approach to market development has proved to be particularly viable, especially for the larger, in-place service organization. However, this concept is tactically limited in that it requires a partnering firm which is not interested in building a service force of its own in the long run.

Service Partnering Relationships

Under the strategic service concept described above, in which the service organization attempts to provide a full, integrated capability to meet a broad array of customer-oriented service requirements and needs, the service organization needs to be able to rapidly develop additional capabilities. Four types of strategic service partnering relationships exist:

- *Technical or logistics partnering*, in which a service organization establishes an arrangement with a manufacturer to obtain parts, technical diagnostics, and training and logistics support

- *Horizontal integration*, in which two or more service organizations with essentially the same capabilities, but with different focuses on products or technology, join together under a single agreement in order to offer integrated, single-point-of-contact service to customers

- *Vertical integration*, in which service organizations with different capabilities or orientations operate together in order to provide customers with a full array of services, such as design, engineering, delivery, installation, maintenance and repair, and training

- *Marketing integration*, in which a sales or distribution organization possessing a strong image or presence within a vertical market segment partners with another organization capable of providing service and support

The four major partnering alternatives outlined above provide an array of options to meet customers' increasing service needs and requirements *without* making a major investment or incurring risk in the development of service marketing capabilities, parts, skills, and diagnostics.

Emerging Opportunities for Partnering Strategies in High-Tech Markets

There are significant and growing opportunities for effective partnering strategies in the service market. Particular market needs which can be effectively met through the strategic service partnering approach include:

- *Requirements for integrated, single-point-of-contact site service.* I have already pointed out that customers are increasingly interested in dealing with a single service vendor in order to avoid finger pointing and significantly improve the ability to identify problems, to improve overall service response and repair time, and to control total maintenance and repair costs through a single contract. This is particularly true with respect to network services involving complex and sophisticated terminals, switches, and peripheral devices. At the present time, for example, most service organizations do not possess the capability for servicing both voice and data technology. A partnering approach between a voice-oriented service organization and a data-oriented service organization could provide an effective solution.

- *Development and integration of complex systems.* There are increasing customer needs for a single vendor to provide complete capabilities for design, engineering, installation, and maintenance and repair for large, complex systems. While many organizations have specific capabilities for design, engineering, and installation, they generally do not offer after-sales maintenance and repair. Alternatively, other organizations provide maintenance and repair capabilities but are not involved in design and installation services. A partnering relationship can bring together these two sets of skills in a single systems integration package that can be offered on a turnkey basis to customers.

- *Multivendor equipment acquisition and deployment.* A third emerging customer requirement involves situations in which a user would like to purchase special or unique hardware, or software, or a mix of hardware available at an extremely low price, or refurbished equipment but is concerned about the after-sales service and support. A partnering relationship between a distributor or value-added systems integrator and a service organization offering full maintenance and repair capabilities could fully meet customer needs and expectations.

As these market requirements and needs regarding full, integrated strategic service increase, the opportunities for strategic partnering will continue to expand.

Requirements for Developing a
Successful Partnering Relationship

Experience has indicated that the most successful partnering relationships in strategic service result from the careful and proactive development of a service marketing plan that is focused on specific customer segments. Market research into those segments provides explicit information on the requirements for integrated service and willingness to pay. The most advantageous partnering opportunities will occur in situations involving a high-density installed base with a high value in use for service. These criteria will ensure a reasonable profit distribution for both partners. Strategic service partnering should also be developed proactively on a long-term basis rather than driven by specific short-term targets of opportunity.

Finding effective partners for strategic service is much easier within the context of such an approach. Typically, the best partners will be ones which can offer:

1. A full understanding of the service opportunities under consideration from both a marketing and technical standpoint

2. The ability to act in a prime and/or subcontract relationship

3. Previous experience in partnering or joint ventures

4. Sophisticated marketing and sales experience

Probably the most important requirement in developing a successful long-term partnering relationship is the existence of mutual advantage for both partners. If the relationship produces significantly higher revenues and profit margins for one of the partners, or if the partnering agreement creates a competitive advantage for only one of the partners, the less-favored partner will tend to be less enthusiastic and will also search for offsetting returns. Thus to ensure success in a partnering relationship, both partners should be *similar in size* and behavioral orientation, and both partners should gain a *mutually equivalent advantage*.

A partnering relationship between a small organization and a major corporation is only rarely successful, and even then only if the personalities in both organizations are heavily committed and take unusual care. Differences in operating style and practices, particularly the larger firm's bureaucratic tendency toward risk aversion in both marketing and pricing, make it extremely difficult for a small organization to partner with a larger one in a situation in which the smaller organization takes the lead role. In addition, in those partnering relationships in which the larger organization takes the lead role, the smaller organization often finds that its own commitment regarding marketing and business development resources is too large relative to the end result which is achieved.

In substance, successful partnering requires that both entities be similar in size; have the same behavioral orientation, understanding of service opportunities, and commitment; and enjoy mutual benefits. Obviously, a written contract can provide the basic framework in which a partnering relationship operates. However, the true business development benefits of partnering occur where the operations are efficient and where the immediate returns ensure positive cooperation with a single face toward the customer, without regard to a written agreement. Strategic service partnering can provide the resources needed to take advantage of the growing opportunities in single-point-of-contact service management and network systems integration without the inherent investment or risk. Also, partnering relationships can be developed to meet a variety of customer needs and requirements.

Summary—Emerging Market Opportunities

The total-service market is growing at a compounded annual rate of more than 20 percent. It is a market where few organizations have operated strategically for more than 10 years. In addition, except in specific market segments (such as computers), there are no *dominant competitors* in the marketplace. This rapid market growth and lack of industry leaders make entry relatively easy for the small entrepreneurial firms. Ease of entry also exists because of the relatively low investment and high return on investment and profit margins found in high-tech service. The service market is also very attractive to larger corporations with existing service operations and those which are expanding their present service operations into the third-party service areas through acquisitions, mergers, or internal growth. In addition, the potential for pulling through product sales has made the service market attractive, particularly for existing service organizations.

I estimate that over the next five years, the high-tech service market will continue to grow. The greatest and most profitable opportunities will be in the deregulated telecommunications and network services marketplace, and organizations that develop portfolios for key vertical market segments will benefit most from these opportunities. Through increased economies of scale, the independent-service approach is a vehicle for growth for existing high-tech firms with service organizations and for firms interested in achieving higher profit margins from their service business.

Typically, growth for existing service organizations is limited, since they usually depend upon their product sales to generate the service revenue base. Entering the independent-service market is the basis for increasing service volume, as well as installed-base density, which in turn can lead to higher profit margins. The most profitable growth opportunities exist for the independent and manufacturer-owned service organizations which can develop and implement sophisticated strategies focused on:

- The service needs and requirements of key *vertical market* segments
- A highly dense customer base with a *high value in use* for service

A service strategy based on vertical market segmentation allows the service organization to:

- *Fine-tune service offerings*, particularly with respect to service needs and requirements and service delivery time
- Enter a market and then use economies of scale and knowledge of user applications to *erect economic and technical barriers* to competitors

The independent-service market is already large, and as it continues to grow, it will offer significant economic opportunities to those suppliers who can and will follow a strategic approach for providing service.

3

Running Service as a Strategic Line of Business

A General Economic Model of the Service Firm

The traditional view of providing service as a cost of doing business has given way, over the past few years, to growing recognition of the need to manage, control, and direct service strategically as a profit center or full line of business. This is a result of pressure from customers who are demanding cost-effective, high-quality service and the growing recognition by business of the contribution of service revenues and service profits to the total corporate account. However, this new requirement for a focus on service has created significant problems for both the executive managing the service aspect of the business and the financial and marketing executives who have, in the typical organization, viewed service as a single cost item in the context of a *product-based* economic model of the firm.

The general economic model of the firm—which defines most cost-accounting, profit analysis, and revenue and cost allocation mechanisms in today's industries—*presumes* the existence of some "product" or "unit of goods" which is produced as a result of the combination of material and labor and which is sold on a *per-unit* basis. The typical product-oriented economic model of the firm is shown in Fig. 3-1a. This model is not precise enough for determining the true economics and profitability of service or for effectively managing and controlling a service

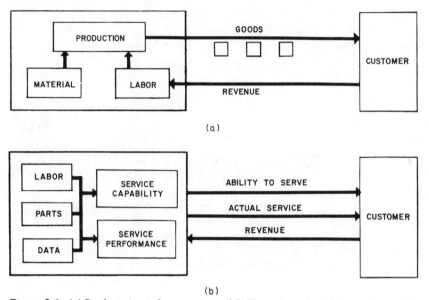

(a)

(b)

Figure 3-1. (a) Product-oriented economic model; (b) service-oriented economic model.

business. A more appropriate *service-based* economic model is shown in Fig. 3-1b for comparison.

The service-based firm primarily utilizes *labor, parts, and data* to provide both a *service capability* on a timely basis and the *actual service performance.* In the service model, the *capability to produce* can generate revenues directly, even though there is no apparent production of a "unit of service." A good example of capability as an economic value involves the Maytag repairman who sits waiting for failure to occur. In the product-oriented economic model this waiting time is viewed as unproductive time. In the service-oriented economic model, this time is not only productive but also *essential* to providing quality service.

The very significant differences between a product business and a service business require a new differentiated conceptual model of the firm, including the financial and accounting processes, for effectively managing the business. These differences, outlined in Table 3-1, are based on the fact that products can be stocked or inventoried, while services cannot; that services are time-sensitive, while products are not; etc. As we shift to managing service strategically, there is a very clear need to fully understand these differences and the specific impact on service operations which results when an attempt is made to use a "standard" model of the firm based on a product orientation.

Table 3-1. Primary Economic, Financial, and Accounting Differences between Product and Service Businesses

Factor or issue in existing product-oriented economic models	Impact on service operations
Products can be stocked or inventoried; services cannot.	How to value "unused" service, assigned to the capability to serve
Service is time-sensitive; products are not.	How to value time (coverage and responsiveness)
Service is viewed as a *component* of product sales.	How to value and control service as a stand-alone line of business How to transfer service price to product lines
A high percentage of service materials and parts can be recycled; product materials and parts are used only once.	How to value and depreciate new and refurbished parts
It is easy to consolidate the costs of materials for products but not for service.	Need for hierarchical structure to evaluate cost allocation of service
There is a higher degree of discretionary expense in service and a lesser degree in manufacturing operations.	More difficult to analyze variable costs of service

Differences between Product- and Service-Oriented Models of the Firm

As indicated above, the use of a product-oriented economic model of the firm to manage, control, and direct service operations can lead to very significant differences in both business strategy and investment allocation. The results of my work with more than 100 corporate organizations show that top management generally views service as both a necessary evil and an increasingly uncontrollable cost of operation.

In addition, most of the normal management theories and practices tend to either not work or be at variance with market conditions and requirements in a service business as opposed to a product business. For example, most executives tend to be reluctant to make any type of investment in service operations, believing that returns are marginal, at best. Service is generally viewed as being a cost or, at best, a breakeven operation.

However, pragmatic evidence suggests that this perception is simply not correct. In a study of 50 product- and 50 service-based firms, my research showed that service-oriented firms have a higher profit before

Table 3-2. Comparison of Typical Product and Service Business Ratios

Key parameters	Product businesses, %	Service businesses, %
Revenue	100	100
Gross margin	45	45
Research and development cost	10–15	1–2
Corporate overhead and general and administration costs	20–30	15
Profit before taxes	6–12	20–30
Return on assets	7–15	70–80

SOURCE: D. F. Blumberg & Associates studies of 100 industrial product and service companies.

taxes than product-based firms (Table 3-2). The higher profit level is due in part to a lower research and development cost as well as lower overhead and general and administration costs as a percentage of gross revenues. Perhaps most interesting is the major difference between product and service firms regarding the return on assets. It is not at all unreasonable to find service businesses generating a 70 to 80 percent return per year, while the return on assets of the typical product-oriented business is only 7 to 15 percent per year. My data suggest that service businesses can generate a far greater return on assets and research and development than product businesses.

Problems with Using a Product-Oriented Model in a Service Firm

Probably the most important issue in using a product-oriented economic model to manage service operations is the tendency to evaluate service on the basis of product factors. This results in the following problems.

Tendency to Reduce Labor-Intensive Activities. The general view of most product-oriented senior managers and corporate executives is that labor-intensive activities are "bad" business and therefore should be reduced or eliminated. Unfortunately, while it is desirable to reduce certain labor-intensive activities in service operations, the primary key to service is the labor content. It is, in fact, the labor portion of the service activity which provides the framework in which actual service is delivered. Thus attempts to cut back on the labor content of service—for example, by eliminating positions or reducing wages—will directly or indirectly lead to a reduction of service quality and capability.

Service capability (i.e., the ability to serve) is often viewed as unproductive. However, the very act of eliminating service positions may cut directly into the "muscle" of the service organization, although the corporate executives may think that it is simply a reduction in the "fat." This is particularly true in the case of those service personnel who provide the capability to perform, i.e., those waiting for customers to arrive in order to provide responsive service. While it appears easy to reduce or eliminate this unproductive labor (in the context of the product-oriented economic model), the real impact is to directly increase the waiting time for customers requesting service.

Tendency to Use Product-Oriented Cost-Plus Pricing Strategies. The impact of the use of a product-oriented economic model in managing service is most directly observed in pricing. The optimum pricing strategy for a product-oriented firm is to charge the lowest manufacturer cost plus a normal markup for overhead and profit. As discussed earlier, service should be priced on the basis of value in use. With this approach it is necessary to determine the real value to the customer or end user of the combination of *the ability to serve* and *actual service.*

Difficulty of Managing Service as a Separate Line of Business. The product-oriented economic model tends to view service as merely an *element* of goods production and delivery. While this might be acceptable in the introduction and growth stages of the product life cycle, pragmatic evidence clearly indicates that as the mature stage is reached, the customer begins to see service as an item that is separate from the product and tends to negotiate both service quality and service price as separable items. In particular, as the installed base of equipment grows, the service opportunity dimensions change very significantly and become an increasingly important framework for the direct generation of revenue and profit, as well as a mechanism for long-term market control.

Incorrect Management of Service Investment and Profit Margins. The use of a product-oriented model in managing service does have one very interesting consequence. When overhead costs are fully allocated to the product and service on the basis of revenues and service (particularly for warranty and installation) is transferred at a market or discounted price, service is generally shown to be very profitable and generates a higher return on assets than found in product businesses. In fact, investment in service can generally be returned in one to two years' time. As I pointed out earlier, a comparison of key parameters for the typical product and service businesses (Table 3-2) clearly indicates that service can be a *very attractive* line of business.

Suggested Service-Based Strategic Approaches

In general, a number of key service management issues such as optimum organization and operating structure, service pricing, and service marketing strategy can be driven in widely varying directions. I will discuss below the impact of these factors on service strategy development.

Organizational Trends in the Service Function

The increasing recognition of the importance of service as both *an independent source of revenues* and a key mechanism for *influencing product sales and market share* has increased the level of strategic thinking regarding the field service function. Partly in response to these pressures, a large number of service organizations have been established as profit centers. They operate as separate divisions or independent subsidiaries,* generally organized centrally, with full key functions, including field operations, finance and administration, marketing, product planning, personnel and industrial relations, technical support and assistance, education, and materials and logistics.

Changes in Strategic Planning in the New Service Organizations

Strategic planning for service operations is also changing. Historically, planning for service in most firms tended to be short-term and tactical in focus, primarily oriented toward the establishment of operating budgets for the next year. The typical planning process in the service organization is still generally based on the establishment and approval of a "reasonable level" of service to achieve a targeted or "general" level of customer satisfaction. Strategic thinking beyond achieving a feasible and/or acceptable service plan was rare or nonefficient because of a lack of understanding of the key factors which affected the future direction of service as a line of business in a typical corporation. This is now changing as the new service organizations begin to focus on the key fac-

---

*This is different from the concept of a cost or contribution center, generally organized under the marketing or sales function.

tors influencing an optimal strategy for a service operation and to identify the elements which could affect the overall service strategy plan.

Factors Affecting Service Strategy

Experience thus far with a number of small, medium, and large service organizations operating in support of product-manufacturing or distribution firms or as independent service businesses clearly shows that there are at least three critical issues which must be considered in the development of a strategic service business plan.

Organizational and Operational Structure of Services.   Service can be viewed merely as a mechanism for influencing sales through customer satisfaction. However, as discussed earlier, service also has considerable value as a source of revenue and profits; in addition, it has considerable value in *pulling through* future product and service sales. These objectives, outlined in Table 3-3, will dictate specific operational goals and, in turn, directly affect the choice of organizational and operational structure.

As the operational goals move from simply supporting sales to managing the full set of values associated with service (e.g., sales support,

Table 3-3. Service Objectives

Strategic objectives	Supporting tactics
Meet customer needs for service; satisfy customers' perceived and actual requirements.	Provide specific services and service-related products: Installation Initial warranty Maintenance and repair Remote diagnostics Moves and changes Training Documentation Software Parts and supplies Depot or rehabilitation
Generate revenues and profits.	Set service portfolio prices above or at cost.
Support or generate future sales.	Identify new customer requirements, and create new service or product opportunities. Provide management data on service performance versus customer requirements.

revenue and profit generation, and market control), it is increasingly necessary to organize and operate service as an independent profit center and line of business and to operate centrally. In summary, the form of service organization and operating structure is dictated to a large extent by the primary objectives of service, as viewed by senior management.

Service-Product Cross Elasticity of Demand.   In most organizations, particularly those in which service historically has been viewed as a support for the sale and marketing of products, a critically important question is the relationship between service and product demand. Possible demand relationships are shown in Fig. 3-2. The specific issue is whether or not there is a high degree of elasticity of demand between the prime product (or service) and the support services per se. For the particular markets and products of interest (to the firm), does the separate sale of services *increase, not affect,* or *decrease* general product sales? This issue has considerable strategic importance in the design of the service strategy and business plan. These demand relationships can be measured through both market research and pilot testing in the field. If there is a strong relationship between product and service demand, then it is more advantageous to tie the service to the product. On the other hand, if the customer prefers to buy the product separate from the service (or has other service options available), then clearly services should be offered separately.

Service Price Elasticity of Demand.   A third major issue relates to the value in use and elasticity of demand as a function of service price to the customer. Possible price-demand relationships are shown in Fig. 3-3. Is

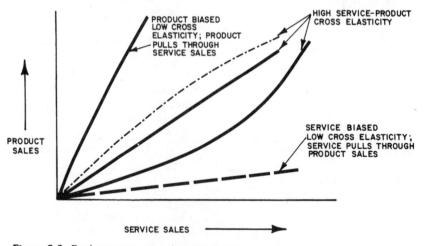

Figure 3-2. Product-service cross elasticity alternatives.

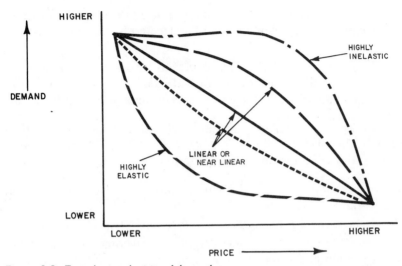

Figure 3-3. Typical price elasticity of demand.

the service customer, particularly in the end-user market, less or more sensitive to price versus quality of service capability and performance? For some customers, concern over service capability and performance is *not critical*; price is the key factor (high price elasticity). For other customers, service capability and performance is the *primary* factor (low price elasticity). Service price elasticity of demand will affect service strategy through its direct impact on both revenues and profit margins that can be associated with operating service as a separate line of business. A high price elasticity (demand changes rapidly as a function of price) means that the prices charged must be as low as possible, above the cost of service delivery; *profit margins are therefore low*. A low price elasticity (customers are relatively insensitive to price changes) means that service can be priced on the basis of its value in use to the customer and generally at a much higher level than the cost of service delivery; thus there is generally a *high profit margin*.

Elements of the Service Strategy Plan

The service strategy plan must first identify the primary objectives of the product or service business with respect to:

1. *The dimensions of the services or products* to be supported and offered (e.g., the types of services). This will be affected by the service-product cross elasticity of demand, driven either by product-related services or directly by service requirements.

2. *The desired level of service revenue and profit and the expected profit margin*These elements will be affected by price elasticity issues.

3. *Levels of support and customer service* to be offered. A firm must know how much service is to be provided as a function of time and coverage. This will be affected by market needs and requirements.

The service strategy plan must also deal with the specific objectives relating to the overall value of service to the firm and the customer base. The strategy must define and describe the following:

1. *Service portfolio to be offered,* including installation, maintenance and repair, moves and changes, etc.

2. *Extension or special coverage services to be offered,* including 24-hour, 7-day-a-week coverage; remote diagnostics coverage; parts availability; education and training service; etc.

3. *Service delivery objectives* relating to service response and service repair time (within 2 or 4 hours, next day, etc.), service installation time, etc., organized by product line and/or market.

4. *Service efficiency and cost targets* relating to the cost of the service call, the cost of installation, etc.

5. *Key service management parameters* which will be utilized to manage and control the service business. These could include but are not limited to the percentage of calls responded to within the service delivery objectives and the percentage of calls completed which did not require the service agent to return within 48 hours.

In summary, the service strategy plan must deal with (1) overall levels of customer satisfaction to be achieved in terms of quantitative performance, (2) levels of revenue and profit margins to be achieved in terms of absolute and relative percentages, and (3) the management organization, operation, and control mechanisms which are to be used to ensure productivity and efficiency in service operations and to meet overall objectives.

Key Factors Affecting the Successful Implementation of the Service Strategy and Business Plan

How can you pull all the above ideas together to develop and implement a winning service strategy and plan? A number of key factors directly affect the formulation, direction, and implementation of the optimum service business plan and strategy. You must deal specifically with the role of the service organization, customer needs and requirements, the organizational and operational structure of service, and product-service demand relationships. These are discussed in more detail below.

The Role of the Service Organization

Service can be used to achieve several distinct and generally valuable objectives.

1. *It can directly influence the decision to buy and increase product sales and market share.* In most markets—particularly for high-technology products such as computers, medical electronics and healthcare equipment, and industrial equipment such as CAD/CAM systems—the quality of the service provided is an especially important factor in the decision to buy from one vendor versus another. The potential customer examines the available vendors to identify those which can offer required product or service features in the general price range of interest. Except in the case of the early stage of a product's life cycle when only one or a few vendors exist, this preliminary examination will lead to a small set of possible vendor candidates. In general, the potential customer makes the final selection decision on the basis of the perceived level and quality of the vendor's service, particularly the ability to respond and repair in the required time frame.

2. *Service can generate substantial revenues and profits directly.* The second major value of service is the revenues generated for service and service-related functions, as well as the profit contribution which can be achieved from the revenues. These include service revenues embedded in the initial product price (for installation and warranty service, for example) and the continuing service revenues from annual maintenance and repair, moves and changes, upgrades, etc. Since total service revenues over the product life cycle will be more than twice the initial product acquisition price, the service revenue stream can be substantial.

Typical profit margins in service are 20 to 30 percent (or more) before taxes, which is considerably greater than the profit margins normally associated with products. At this level of profitability, it is assumed that the initial installation and warranty services are paid for by the product or manufacturing division requiring the services at a normal market price. It should be noted that many service organizations normally transfer initial warranty and installation services to the product or manufacturing organization at *cost*, rather than cost plus a normal markup and profit. This has the effect of shifting profit contribution which *should actually appear under the service organization's financial structure* to the product organization. On a fully accounted basis (full service cost allocated against full service price), service revenues and profits will be substantial.

3. *Service can be used to control markets; satisfied service customers will remain with a specific vendor.* The third major value of service is the ability to pull through future product and service sales. This is a result of maintaining a continuing relationship with customers through actual service experience as well as the use of service to support product moves and changes, upgrades, and expansion. In general, satisfied service customers will tend to maintain their relationship with a given vendor rather than risk problems with another service organization. This means a strong tendency to continue to buy *both* products and service from the vendor offering satisfactory service. It is important to note that this pull-through value can be related to both "hard," or tangible, products and "soft," or intangible, items (i.e., training, supplies, software, engineering, technical assistance, etc.).

In summary, as outlined in Table 3-3, there are three critical roles associated with a service business. For the service business operating in the context of a manufacturing organization, all three values exist. For the service organization operating independently (i.e., as a third-party maintainer), all three roles also exist and are critical. For the service business operating in the environment of a product organization, a decision must be made as to which of these roles exist. The most comprehensive strategy will consider all three roles.

Customer Needs and Requirements

The second major factor influencing the general shape of the service strategy is the identification and evaluation of the particular customer service needs and requirements which exist and must be met. Extensive market studies clearly show that the customer places the highest emphasis on service response and repair *times,* installation *times,* etc. There is a high correlation between the ability to deliver service within a given or desired *time frame* and *satisfaction* with service. Customer dissatisfaction levels can increase sharply if required service is not provided. In effect, too much service can be just as bad as too little service but for different reasons. We will discuss this issue in much more detail in Chap. 4.

We must recognize, as discussed earlier (in Chap. 1), that different types of customers have different service needs. In each specific market segment, the customer has reasonably well defined requirements as to acceptable response and repair times, installation times, etc. As an example, a large multinational bank may have a response requirement of less than 1 hour for maintenance problems associated with its mainframe computers. On the other hand, a retail establishment utilizing a personal computer for sales forecasting might be more than willing to wait more than 48 hours for service response. Thus the *type of product* requiring service, the *market segment*, and the *application of the product or service* all tend to dictate the level of service performance and the time frame for response which a service organization must meet to achieve customer satisfaction.

As I have already shown, service quality is most often measured by the customer at times when the service organization *fails to perform*. Thus it is not so much the *actual* performance but the ability to avoid *critical failures of service performance within targeted time frames* which tends to most heavily influence customer satisfaction levels. For example, the occurrence of a *single* event in which a critically required service is not provided within the time frame required could create a significant drop in the level of customer satisfaction, even though in many past events, service was provided within a reasonable, acceptable time frame. It is the customer's *perception* of service which heavily influences customer satisfaction with service in the field.

A customer's perception of service quality and performance can be heavily influenced either *positively* or *negatively* by *peer comments* and other *secondary sources*. A customer who hears from other users that service quality and performance are very good will be less prone to criticize the random event in which service is not good. On the other hand, if the customer is sensitive to the possibility of poor quality because of other users' comments, the random event of poor service will be viewed as being the more general case.

Customers are generally insensitive to the provision of service at a level which is *significantly more rapid* than required. In fact, there is a *penalty* (i.e., an increase in cost and therefore a reduction of the profit margin) associated with providing *too much* service. This is particularly true because the customer (or potential customer) can easily recognize the absence of service criteria needed but cannot easily observe or measure too much service. Thus it is essential to accurately determine customer needs and requirements for service, especially as they relate to time parameters, and then ensure that service is provided to *just meet* those service objectives.

The Organizational and Operational Structure of Service

The third major factor which influences the implementation of the service strategy and business plan is the organizational and operational structure of service.

Organizational Structure.   Three types of organizational structure can be used for financial control: *cost centers, contribution centers*, and *profit centers*. Each form is discussed below.

Cost Centers.   To the extent that influencing product sales is the service value desired, service will generally be organized as a decentralized *cost center* with the greatest focus on simply ensuring customer satisfaction by minimizing complaints at the local level. A cost center is operated as a function of an authorized budget. It does not generate revenues or profit. In general, this type of organization will tend to reduce the potential of the second and third values (direct generation of revenues and profits and market control due to the ability to pull through future sales).

Contribution Centers.   A second form of service organization is a *contribution center*, which is normally operated under marketing. This organization typically focuses on the product support and market control values of service. A contribution center may be organized as a budget center or a profit center, but it is operated tactically in support of the market function or other functions to which it "contributes." This type of organization generally operates against a budget but also is expected to generate some profit contribution, although not on the basis of a full allocation of costs against revenue.

Independent Profit Centers.   These organizations are designed to generate revenues against costs to produce a full profit. Businesses which stress the *full value* of service usually organize service as a separate line of business—as a profit center or independent subsidiary—and are generally organized on a *centralized* basis. They also tend to be, in general, much more efficient and effective. Perhaps more important, compared with cost centers and contribution centers, the profit centers tend to provide the framework for creating a much more sophisticated service-oriented strategy and business plan, a broader and more appropriate service portfolio, and more effective service pricing.

Operational Structure.   Three types of operational structures have emerged. They provide the basic framework in which service is conducted, managed, and directed.

Centralized Operations.   A centralized service operation is typically organized with a national senior service executive (president or general manager) supported by both a full staff and a director or vice president of field operations, organized into major regions. This type of operation is usually found in the profit-center-oriented service division or subsidiary, as well as in the typical independent service organization or third-party maintenance organization. It appears to be the most efficient operational structure.

Regional Operations. Another typical operational structure of service involves regionally directed service forces. Primary operations are directed at the regional level, with technical support and logistics support being provided.

Local or Decentralized Operations. A third type of operational structure is the decentralized or local form, which involves service management at the branch or district level. Typically, a service unit will report to a sales and marketing organization at the branch or district level. The service force is backed up by technical and logistics staff functions.

Product-Service Demand Relationships

I have already pointed out that a key strategic issue is whether, in a given market and for a given product or service, the manufactured product or service primarily pulls through additional *service demand* (i.e., product-biased low cross elasticity of demand), whether the support service pulls through the original *product* or general service *demand* (i.e., service-biased low cross elasticity of demand), or whether there is an element of *independence* between the initial product or service and the demand for support service. The general hypothesis of most industrial marketing and sales executives is that a demand relationship exists between product and service and that it is highly *product-biased*. In fact, many marketing executives are concerned about the general concept of service being provided as an independent line of business or profit center because they feel that the availability of service independent of the product would reduce product sales; presumably, the potential customer might buy the service from one organization but the tangible product from another vendor because of a lower price or better features.

Unfortunately, most firms have done little quantitative market research on this subject. Organizations should recognize that this issue is particularly relevant to the concept of running service as a strategic line of business.

Market surveys make it possible to measure this cross elasticity of demand. Customers can be asked whether they prefer to buy service and product together or separately. They can also be asked whether buying one could lead to buying the other from the same or a different vendor. An alternative way of determining the existence or absence of product-service cross elasticity of demand is to test-market different concepts in different areas. In one area products can be sold independently of service; in another area products and service can be combined. Differences in demand under different service and product offering strategies can then be measured. I will discuss market survey approaches in Chap. 4.

Actual Product-Service Cross Elasticity of Demand

The limited market research on the subject of product-service cross elasticity of demand indicates that there is a high degree of such demand, particularly in mature markets and industries, and that the demand is generally more *service-biased* than product-biased. The data suggest that there is a significantly higher demand for quality service offered *independently*.

In addition, the data suggest that quality service will often *pull through* product sales. Given a choice between vendors, customers will prefer to buy a product from their preferred *service* vendor, even though the price of the product may be much higher and the product features less desirable. Market studies show that while some segments of any market are sensitive to product features or product prices, a significantly larger percentage of the general market is less concerned about these issues, so long as the product is capable of performing to meet business requirements. Customers are much more concerned about service quality and performance. Thus the availability of high-quality service as a separate line of business will serve to generate an increase in both service revenues and product revenues.

This is particularly true with respect to future product purchases. While the typical salesperson may not be able to convince a customer to shift from one vendor's manufactured products to another, he or she may be able to capture the service business separately. With service performance comes increased loyalty to the alternative vendor. Then, at the next upgrade or modification, there is a tendency to make use of the service vendor's *product lines* through the loyalty value of service. Thus the availability of service as a *separate* line of business offers a dual opportunity to make a sale, whereas provision of service only as a tactical support for product sales limits the sales opportunity.

The Strategic Role of Service as a Line of Business

In summary, my analysis and very extensive market research suggest that all firms should view service as a strategic business unit. A proactively developed service-oriented strategy focused on providing a full service portfolio to meet customer needs and requirements will significantly increase *revenues and profit margins* in both the short and the long run, significantly improve *market position and control,* and *augment* rather than reduce product sales. This strategy, if properly managed and executed, has a very significant chance of *prevailing,* whereas the typical product-oriented strategy, with service being utilized in tactical support of sales, is considerably less powerful. This is especially true if the service function is operating at a high level of productivity.

Steps in Examining the Factors Affecting Service Strategy

In developing your own service strategy, you need to ask the following questions in order to best determine whether service should be organized and operated as an independent line of business, as a dependent cost center, or as a contribution center supporting broad marketing goals and objectives.

1. *Is there a positive, negative, or neutral demand relationship between product and service?* Will the offering of service as an independent line of business affect product sales (both in general and in specific markets) positively, negatively, or not at all? Market research data suggest very strongly that in many markets, particularly mature industries, service can be sold independently without negatively affecting product sales. In many situations it can actually serve to *increase* both total product and total service sales. If service has a positive or neutral effect on product sales, it is better to offer it to the customer base on an independent basis.

2. *Is service demand affected significantly, a little, or not at all by a change in price?* A second important question is whether or not a firm can *significantly* increase its revenues and profit margins from the sale of service by raising prices. Usually, service is priced on a cost-plus basis; in some markets pressure is placed by marketing management to reduce service prices in order to sell products. Market research suggests that a significant percentage of industrial-product users are willing to pay a *premium* (i.e., a higher price) for better service than they are currently receiving. Customers are usually less sensitive to a price change than to a change in service quality, particularly if the service vendor emphasizes service quality differences. In terms of the perceived *quality* of service, demand is relatively inelastic with respect to price. Thus there is a *significant* opportunity for service providers to *increase revenues* and *profit margins* where service users are much more quality-sensitive than

price-sensitive. The service providers can expand and improve the service portfolio and reprice it on the basis of value in use.

3. *Can the service force improve its productivity?* If a firm aggressively expands its service business, it should realize the importance of improving its ability to deliver the additional service without a concurrent increase in costs. Management action to improve productivity through more efficient call dispatch and logistics can increase service business profit margins to a level of at least 20 to 30 percent before taxes. If the service organization is not this productive, it should be managed more centrally as a separate line of business.

By asking and answering these three questions, executives and managers can recognize those situations in which a service-based strategy will be much more effective and productive than a product-based strategy. The answers to these questions will also help determine the best way to manage and control service.

Appropriate market research should be conducted to directly measure the service-product cross elasticity of demand and determine whether offering service as an independent line of business would in any way reduce the sale of products. In the case of such a finding, it would be a simple matter to limit independent service business to those areas where it does not directly compete with the existing products or where the firm has a significant market share.

I also strongly urge a quantitative examination of *service price elasticity* as a basis for introducing new services and pricing in order to generate significantly higher service revenues and profit margins.

In general, my studies suggest that service should be marketed, distributed, and priced as a *separate line of business* in markets which have:

High service-product cross elasticity of demand

High value in use for service

Service-biased low cross elasticity of demand

Service should be used strategically in *support* of product sales in markets which have:

Low service-product cross elasticity of demand

Low value in use for service

Product-biased low cross elasticity of demand

Executives need to recognize that service as a separate line of business is an extremely viable concept—one that can be fully synergistic with most firms' present commitments in their markets. Service can also be used to support product sales. However, even in this specialized situation, service needs to be managed *strategically*. In both situations, it is necessary to fully understand the costs and profits associated with service operations.

Steps in Establishing Service-Oriented Accounting and Financial Controls

I have already shown that there are real differences between the product-oriented economic model of a firm and the new service-oriented economic model. The true costs and profitability of service can be highly visible when specific service-oriented financial and accounting mechanisms are created within the firm. Executives and managers must take action to produce:

1. *A formal service-oriented accounting structure* for collecting all costs associated with the elements of service operations, including labor, parts, data, and related support for both field maintenance and depot maintenance and repair.

2. *A new accounting line item allowing for the direct measurement of* service capability *or* the ability to serve. This line item cost is to be associated with revenues related to the ability to deliver premium or superior service quality and responsiveness.

3. *The separation of service revenues from product revenues and formal price transfer mechanisms based on market price* to reflect the service organization's delivery of service in support of installation and initial warranty activities. Typically, if the charges for these activities are currently transferred from the service organization to a product or distribution organization, they are transferred at cost, and this creates what appears to be an excessive cost ratio in the service organization and an excessive profit representation in the product organization.

4. *Formalization of pricing of the service portfolio to include price and cost differentials* associated with different levels of service response and performance. In effect, the requirement is to develop a service portfolio (similar to a product portfolio) for the service business.

5. *A formal service business and marketing strategy and an operational plan.*

6. *Formal parameters for evaluating service profitability and return on assets* on the basis of a comparison with service industry and market

standards rather than product-oriented standards. As indicated earlier, a typical service business return on assets (ROA) can run from 70 to 80 percent per year versus a product business ROA in the range of 7 to 15 percent. Profit before taxes in service can run from 20 to 30 percent versus 6 to 12 percent for product-oriented businesses. It is important to recognize that these profit levels and ROA figures are correct, although they appear to be significantly higher than the typical product performance. Thus service should be evaluated on exactly the same measures as a product business but with the recognition that the service ROI and profit margins represent *real economic alternatives* and are not just the result of anomalies in the accounting system.

In summary, service should be managed and run strategically, either as a separate line of business or in support of product lines. In either case the service executive must create financial and accounting structures and a management system based upon a recognition of the key differences between the product-oriented and service-oriented economic models of the firm. Through the implementation of service-oriented financial and accounting mechanisms which reflect these differences, management can truly control both product and service businesses on a structured basis.

4

Providing Customers with What They Want

Understanding the Customer's Process of Selection

As the service industry becomes increasingly concerned with the development and implementation of an effective and efficient organization to provide service as a profitable line of business, increasing focus is being placed on the measurement, control, and delivery of customer and field service to fully satisfy market requirements and needs. Historically, there has always been interest in improving satisfaction with service in much the same way that there has been interest in motherhood and apple pie. However, the typical marketing and service executives have never seriously investigated or understood the underlying mechanisms for measuring customer satisfaction with service, nor have they been willing to carry out appropriate research and development to implement a quantitative, objective mechanism for the measurement and control of customer satisfaction.

In today's business environment, the ability to deliver optimized customer and field service at a profit is no longer of trivial concern. For example, the maturing of the typical information technology product, coupled with the increasing dependence of users on the array of information technology equipment installed on site to support day-to-day operations, has caused that marketplace to emphasize service quality and delivery as never before.

Market studies carried out for almost every type of product in every market and industry segment have *consistently* established the fact that most customers utilize their perceptions of service satisfaction levels, in terms of responsiveness and the capability to deliver. These perceived satisfaction levels are a *critical factor* in their decision to buy products as well as service from one vendor versus another.

The Two-Step Selection Process

The potential buyer of a product or service normally uses a two-step approach in selecting a vendor.

1. *Determination of purchase parameters.* The first step in the decision to buy is to define the form, fit, and function of the product or service required, on the basis of internal needs and future objectives. In this process, the upper and lower budget limits are also established. The customer defines the minimum amount he or she is willing to pay for the product or service which meets the form, fit, and function requirements. The customer also establishes the maximum economic value beyond which he or she will not go. Having established these parameters, the potential buyer will then search for the vendor or vendors who will satisfy his or her needs. Normally, for any product or service line which is in the growth or maturing stage, this search will result in the identification of *at least* two or three potential vendors.

It should be noted that in the introductory stage of the life cycle of a product or service, the buyer might find only a *single* vendor, either because only one vendor has developed the required form, fit, and function within the price range desired or because the potential buyer does not have enough knowledge of the marketplace to be able to find more than one vendor. In this special case, the purchaser will decide to buy or not to buy from that vendor.

2. *Final vendor selection.* Assuming that in the first step the potential buyer has identified two or more vendors who can meet the form, fit, function, and budget requirements, he or she then proceeds to evaluate and compare those vendors. In general, unless the buyer is extremely price-sensitive or is driven by legal or defined procurement rules and regulations toward the lowest bidder, the vendor who is finally selected will be the one who is *perceived* as offering the highest-quality customer and field service which satisfies the buyer's needs and requirements. If a product is involved, this purchase analysis will usually include a trade-off between product reliability (and/or maintainability) and after-sale service and support.

Because of the two-step approach, *product quality and reliability alone* will not guarantee a final vendor selection, since the user is usually aware of the fact that there is no possibility of an infinite interval between failures. In essence, the purchaser will generally recognize that the product or service *will fail to perform* at some point in time, and at that juncture the quality of service response and fault correction will be critical. In the final analysis, in the second step a positive perception of service satisfaction and quality will generally lead to positive vendor selection.

The Impact of Life-Cycle Stage

Understanding this two-step vendor selection process, including the importance of customer *perceptions* of service satisfaction, is critical to understanding service requirements and needs. Service requirements and needs always exist; however, they become more important in the later stages of the life cycle; then service becomes essential to customers, who use it either directly or in support of maturing product lines. Thus a product or technology follower can, over the life cycle, dominate its market through strategic service delivery. Service vendors who can fine-tune their service portfolio to meet customer requirements or who can focus on customer perceptions for service and then create the capability to meet these new service demands can also dominate in their markets. The typical approach of reducing price as competition increases may be superseded by the delivery of quality services. In this case, a vendor can maintain a higher price, except for those segments of the marketplace which are highly price-sensitive or forced by procurement regulations or policy legislation to choose the lowest bidder.

Meeting Customer Requirements for Service

The process described above, which suggests that the perception of service quality and customer satisfaction is the *most important factor* in the final vendor selection, is demonstrated in market survey after market survey. Table 4-1 presents the results of four separate and totally independent customer surveys regarding different high-tech products.* Purchasers were asked to rate the importance of various factors that affect the final selection of a vendor. Product reliability and perceived service performance (defined in terms of operating quality of product after repair) ranked highest on the list on a scale of 1 to 5, with 1 standing for "most important." Thus service and service-related factors can and, in fact, do dominate other important considerations such as price of

---

*These surveys were all done by mail. They involved 300 to 400 responses from a universe randomly selected from the user base of the individual products.

Table 4-1. Results of Four Independent Customer Surveys

Ratings of Factors of Importance in the Decision to Select a Particular Vendor's Product*

Factors	Product type			
	A	B	C	D
Price of product	2.56	2.90	2.70	2.34
Reliability of product	(1.28)	(1.49)	(1.44)	(1.69)
Price of service	2.70	2.88	2.98	2.81
Operating quality of product after repair	(1.75)	(1.74)	(1.55)	(1.82)
Previous experience with vendor	3.53	3.57	3.41	3.94
Reputation of vendor	2.85	2.75	3.27	3.35
Product features	2.62	2.45	2.98	3.63
Timely delivery of product	2.71	2.60	3.46	3.87
Service time	(1.42)	(1.69)	(1.87)	(2.04)
Price of supplies	3.18	3.07	3.05	2.44
Product operating capability	3.19	2.54	2.98	3.07
Ease of product operation	2.06	2.38	2.52	2.61

*A scale of 1 to 5 was used; 1 is the highest value. Note that the three most important factors are circled in each column and coincide across the four product types.

SOURCE: D. F. Blumberg & Associates studies of service markets.

product, product features, and even service price. In a survey concerning any one of the products, the same customers were asked to rate (on the same scale of 1 to 5) the ability of major vendors to perform, using the same factors of importance (as shown in Table 4-2). The typical survey suggests that the vendor *ranked the best on service-related factors* (in this particular case, vendor 2) will *always have* the *highest market share* or will have *the most rapid growth*. In essence, there is an extremely high correlation between customer satisfaction with service performance and market share.

In summary, customer satisfaction with service is not only important but also *absolutely critical* to both the service organizations supporting tangible-product sales and the service organizations operating as independent lines of business. Service-oriented vendors increasingly dominate the market, particularly for products in the growth or maturing stage of the life cycle. In addition, for a very high percentage of the market, a high level of customer satisfaction can often overcome, or at least compensate for, higher prices.

Table 4-2. Individual-Product Customer Survey
Ratings of Competitive Vendors' Abilities to Meet Customers' Needs*

Factors	Competitors 1	2	3	4
Price of product	(2.00)	▽2.73	2.04	2.66
Reliability of product	▽3.37	(2.00)	2.16	2.32
Price of service	▽2.76	(2.38)	2.43	2.56
Operating quality of product after repair	▽2.68	1.93	2.55	(1.83)
Previous experience with vendor	▽2.56	(2.12)	2.54	2.24
Reputation of vendor	2.21	1.67	▽2.27	(1.62)
Product features	2.56	2.20	▽2.87	(2.11)
Timely delivery of product	2.22	2.25	(2.10)	▽2.56
Service time	▽2.83	(2.12)	2.21	2.42
Price of supplies	▽3.06	(2.59)	2.68	2.64
Product operating capability	▽2.39	(1.87)	2.21	2.02
Ease of product operation	1.83	1.82	(1.71)	▽1.92
Market share	14%	39%	26%	21%

*A scale of 1 to 5 was used; 1 is the highest value. Products that performed best in a category are circled. Products that performed worst in a category are marked with a triangle.
SOURCE: D. F. Blumberg & Associates studies of service markets.

Key Measures of Customer Satisfaction

Given that customer satisfaction with service and perceived service quality are critically important, it is necessary to quantitatively measure, manage, control, and deliver service quality. The most important factors in measuring service quality and satisfaction can be determined by returning to the data from the customer surveys. In the same four surveys described above, customers were questioned as to the factors they use in evaluating service quality. Table 4-3 shows that *service response and repair time* and a related *guarantee* of that service time frame (i.e., once the service engineer completes the task, it will not have to be repeated) are the most important factors in evaluating service levels. For every type of product and in every market segment, customers and po-

Table 4-3. Results of Four Independent Customer Surveys
Ratings of Factors of Importance in Evaluating Product Service*

Factors	Product type			
	A	B	C	D
Ability to respond rapidly to a service call	(1.32)	(1.67)	(2.71)	(1.82)
Ability to service all types of products	3.27	3.13	3.34	2.98
Software maintenance	2.18	2.79	2.45	2.82
Resident technician	3.57	3.68	3.82	3.60
Price of service	3.00	3.08	2.91	2.58
Speed of service repair	(1.47)	(1.79)	(1.89)	(1.94)
Professional attitude of service engineer	2.59	2.73	2.79	2.83
Friendliness and courtesy of service engineer	2.67	2.89	2.98	2.93
Technical ability of service engineer to repair the first time	(1.45)	(1.81)	(1.68)	(1.78)

*A scale of 1 to 5 was used; 1 is the highest value. Note that the three most important factors are circled in each column and coincide across the four product types.
SOURCE: D. F. Blumberg & Associates studies of service markets.

tential customers have a specific view of *how much is enough time* to wait for service to be completed.

Shape of the Customer Satisfaction Index

I have already pointed out that satisfaction levels are definitely non-linear and, in fact, closely approximate a step function; the step is typically driven directly by the acceptable-service-time requirements of 70 to 80 percent of the customer base.* The typical customer satisfaction index is directly related to the perceived ability of the individual service organization to meet the service time requirement. It should be noted that this time parameter is the *perceived*, rather than the real, time in any given situation. This is true because customers are extremely sensitive to situations in which they have to wait an excessively long time due to the service organization's failure to respond. Thus their view of service performance is extremely biased. In essence, their perceptions are heavily influenced by those situations in which the service organization *fails to perform* within the time period of importance to them.

The unusual *nonlinear* character of this customer satisfaction index

*See Chap. 1, Fig. 1-4, and pages 20 and 21.

must be clearly understood by the service organization. Most service managers tend to think of the customer satisfaction index as *linear* and *positively directed*; they believe that decreasing service performance time will lead directly to a linear increase in customer satisfaction. In fact, as discussed previously, once the service response and repair time parameter is met, an increased level of responsiveness does not "buy" an increased level of customer satisfaction. It may, in some situations, result in lower levels of perceived customer satisfaction.

Influencing Perceptions of Service Quality

It is important to recognize that service quality is primarily *perceived* and that customer perceptions of service can be highly influenced by service management procedures and practices. For example, if a service organization, in its call-handling procedure, gives a customer an estimated time of arrival of the service engineer (i.e., service response time) at the time of the initial call and then *fails* to meet that time requirement, the customer will perceive service as being of low quality, even though the actual service response time may meet the customer's requirements. For example, at the time a customer calls, if the service organization indicates that the estimated time of arrival (ETA) will be 2 hours and the service engineer arrives in 3 hours, the service quality is regarded as low.

If a customer, at the time of calling in, is given an ETA of 3½ hours and the service engineer arrives in 3 hours, service quality is regarded positively. In essence, an ETA (provided at the time the customer calls in) which is consistently on the low side will create a perception of service quality, and if it is not met, customer dissatisfaction levels will increase substantially. This knowledge suggests that it is undesirable to provide an ETA at the time a customer calls in. However, my service studies in various markets clearly show that customers do desire an ETA at the time they call in. The answer is, of course, to provide an ETA that is based on the actual situation—that is, to calculate the probable response time given the current status of service engineers, travel time, etc. It is also a good idea to be conservative in response time estimates—to err by overestimating rather than setting expectations which are not or cannot be met.

Customer satisfaction is best measured by a nonlinear index which is directly tied to *perceived service completion* (i.e., response and repair time) as compared with the user's required service completion time. It should be clearly noted that it is, in fact, the *total service closure time* which is important to the customer—not just the arrival time or the initiation of service action. Customer perceptions of service are invariably related to the total elapsed time between the initial request for service and the completion of the service task.

Customer Satisfaction and Willingness to Pay

Service executives often become confused when they find that customer satisfaction does not automatically correlate with willingness to pay. Executives often point out that customers are not always willing to pay a higher price for higher levels of service performance. They fail to recognize that not only are there different market segments and different service requirements, but there are also different types of service customers.

There is actually a good correlation between willingness to pay and perceived satisfaction with service. However, this demand relationship is affected in intensity and direction by the factors underlying customer satisfaction levels and willingness to pay. In the first place, it is essential to understand the nonlinear, step nature of customer satisfaction as discussed above. There is a point at which improved service quality does not increase customer satisfaction. In the second place, it is critically important to understand the price sensitivity or elasticity factors in the marketplace. There are at least three types of customers in the marketplace with regard to price:

1. *Price-sensitive customers.* There is a class of customers who are extremely price-sensitive, either because of the nature of their business or because of legislative, policy, or procedural requirements. Government agencies and educational institutions, for example, are particularly price-sensitive because of their own procurement policies. This class of customers places little value on service quality. Their primary criterion is the lowest price. Even a slight change in price relative to competition will cause a change in their buying behavior.

2. *Price-quality customers.* A large percentage of the marketplace (approximately 50 percent) tends to make a *balanced* trade-off between price and quality. The result is a fairly linear relationship between willingness to pay and customer satisfaction for a given purchase decision.

3. *Time- and quality-sensitive customers.* The third class of customers is extremely sensitive to time and service quality and is relatively price-insensitive. For these customers, service is the critical factor, and within reasonable limits they are prepared to pay whatever it takes to get the desired service quality and performance. In fact,

these customers typically want to pay in order to be able to command the service they need.

In essence, customer satisfaction levels can be directly converted to price acceptance and willingness to pay for that segment of the market which properly performs a service price–service quality trade-off. The highly price-sensitive and time- and quality-sensitive customers do not react in the same way. The percentage of customers who fall into these three categories will vary by market segment and product line. However, extensive market studies suggest that in service, the price-quality (or typical) customers usually account for about 50 percent of the market; on the average, 35 to 40 percent of the users are time- and quality-sensitive; and the rest, or 10 to 15 percent, are highly price-sensitive. These findings suggest that it is strategically more desirable to focus on service quality, which is important to 85 to 90 percent of the market, rather than service price, which is important to only 10 to 15 percent of the market.

There is also a *fourth class of customers* who have an unusual attitude with respect to service price. These customers are the less sophisticated buyers for whom price becomes a direct *surrogate* for quality in terms of expected customer satisfaction levels. Some customers have greater difficulty than others in determining the level of customer service satisfaction which vendors offer; they simply lack experience or the ability to perceive customer service directly. This class of customers tends to use *price* as a direct measure of quality; they are often willing to pay a higher price because they believe that this will lead to better service performance.

In summary, in an extremely rational market, where almost all the customers perform a normal price-quality trade-off, there is a high correlation between customer satisfaction and willingness to pay. The existence of the highly price-sensitive (i.e., price-elastic) and time-sensitive (i.e., price-inelastic) customers, as well as the price-surrogate customers (i.e., those who use price as a surrogate for quality), tends to mask or confuse the prevailing relationship.

How to Measure Service Requirements and Needs, Quality, and Customer Satisfaction Levels

From the above analysis, it is quite clear that the experienced service manager should pay a great deal of attention to the measurement of service quality, customer satisfaction levels, and customer needs. Since the satisfaction level is nonlinear and is generally a perceived factor, it is critical to measure levels of customer satisfaction on a regular basis (at least annually), utilizing some form of market research or field survey. The available market research and survey mechanisms, outlined in Table 4-4, include (1) direct personal interviews, (2) focus groups, (3) telephone surveys, (4) mail surveys, and (5) other approaches (telemarketing, mail-in cards). Each of these survey mechanisms offers both advantages and disadvantages in terms of depth of response, statistical validity and comparison, cost, and controllability. These mechanisms vary according to the format used and the sample size.

One of two formats can be used to conduct surveys:

- *Open-ended:* Questions are generally framed, but no answers are defined in advance. A respondent can answer the questions in any terms he or she feels comfortable with.

- *Close-ended:* Questions are more specifically framed, and specific answers are provided. A respondent may pick the best or most applicable answer from the multiple choices offered.

Usually, the best survey mechanism is initially constructed with the open-ended format and is directed at a small sample of customers to define both the questions and the range of acceptable or appropriate answers. From these results a close-ended survey format is developed for use with a large sample.

The sample size of the survey is also critical. In general, the respondents should be drawn at random from the specific universe, or population, of interest (customers, new customers, etc.). The size of the sample should be established to ensure adequate representation of the universe in terms of the size, type, and orientation of the market segments. Typically, the sample can be relatively small, compared with the total population, and still provide valid results. The rule is to have a minimum of 5 to 15 respondents to each question for each subsegment in the survey mechanism. Consider, for example, a questionnaire designed to evaluate service requirements and needs and customer satisfaction levels on the basis of these factors:

Size (3 levels: small, medium, and large)

Type (5 segments)

Geographic region (4 areas)

The survey would require a minimum sample of $3 \times 5 \times 4 = 60$ subsegments, or a minimum sample size of 300 to 900 [$60 \times (5{-}15)$]. This should always be compared with the total universe to ensure that the

Table 4-4. Alternative Survey Mechanisms

Customer satisfaction survey mechanism	General description	Advantages	Disadvantages
In-depth personal interview	1- to 2-hour one-on-one interview with user, using structured or unstructured questions	Ability to obtain detailed information	Expensive Time-consuming Difficult to schedule
Focus group	2- to 3-hour session with 6 to 12 peers in group	Ability to obtain consensus Ability to see the effect of other perceptions	Difficult to administer and control Could be biased by one participant
Full telephone survey	30- to 45-minute telephone interview using structured questionnaire	Ability to obtain unbiased results Ability to control	Somewhat expensive Not easy to compare complex alternatives
Full mail survey	30- to 45-minute structured questionnaire sent out and returned on random basis	Ability to obtain unbiased results Ability to obtain quantitative data on complex alternatives	Expensive Low response rates Not easy to control
Telemarketing and call handling	3- to 5-minute initial call, usually used with call handling	Ease of administering to existing base	Does not test nonclient base
Mail-in cards	Card given to customers by service region at the close of a call	Inexpensive	Does not test nonclient base

sample represents a minimum of 1.0 percent of the total universe for which the survey results will be projected. Thus for a total population of 10,000 customers, a minimum sample of 100 customers would provide valid results. These rules of thumb can generally be applied in most service survey designs to provide reasonable results at a confidence level of 85 to 90 percent. A discussion of specific market research sampling formulas and procedures can be found in many standard market research texts.

Survey Mechanisms

Direct Personal Interviews   Typically, direct personal interviews are based on the open-ended survey format and a relatively small sample size. The value of the interviews depends on the quality, capability, and experience of the interviewer. This process can provide in-depth answers because the interviewer can explore answers to specific questions at the time of the interview. The primary disadvantage is cost. Direct personal interviews are difficult to schedule, particularly to reach senior-level managers and executives, and expensive to administer.

Focus Groups   This survey mechanism involves interviewing customers in a group. Respondents are identified and asked to attend a group meeting at a designated time and place. Usually, some economic incentive ($10 to $20 for an hour session) is offered. A trained interviewer and focus group leader is assigned to coordinate the group. Typically, groups are made up of 6 to 12 respondents; too large a group becomes unwieldy, and too small a group reduces the accuracy of the results. Often the focus group meetings are held in a specially designed conference room: microphones are used to record the discussions, and one-way mirrors allow other observers to "sit in" on the discussions.

The group leader will usually pose each question in an open-ended format. The leader will then attempt to poll the participants to obtain an answer that reflects a consensus.

This approach can be useful in dealing with complex questions, new services, and future trends. The advantages are that the leader can see a consensus formed, and the participants, or peers, can interact and exchange ideas. Disadvantages are that the focus group results are not easily extrapolated to the full universe, and the answers may not be statistically valid or comparable to the results of focus groups held at other times and/or locations.

Telephone Surveys   The telephone survey usually has a close-ended format. Typically, the survey is administered by experienced telephone interviewers, who use computer-aided technology to present the questions and record the answers. There are several advantages to a telephone survey. The survey process makes it possible to reach the right respondent or decision maker. Thus one can be assured that the correct person provides the answers. Also, since the interviewer is on the phone, the respondent can ask for clarification of any question. In addition, the sample size can be managed, since the interviewer knows the *exact* number of respondents at any time. The results can often be tabulated rapidly, especially if a computerized system to support the telephone is used. Usually, the questionnaire is designed to avoid bias in the sequence of both questions and answers provided. "Skip patterns" are used to provide the multiple-choice answers on a random basis. The primary disadvantage of a telephone survey is that it is difficult to ask complex comparison-type questions. In addition, the process can be expensive, although it is much less expensive per respondent than a direct personal interview.

Mail Surveys Mail surveys usually involve a close-ended questionnaire that is sent to a relatively large sample population. The survey must be designed on the basis of the fact that only about 10 to 20 percent of the survey instruments mailed out will be returned. Thus if a response population of 100 is required, approximately 500 to 1000 survey instruments need to be mailed. This response rate can be improved by including or offering an incentive—a gift such as a pen, a dollar bill, or a summary of the survey results. The primary advantage of the mail survey is that it can be used to obtain answers to complex or multipart questions. If properly designed, the mail survey also allows the respondents to answer the questions thoughtfully, and at their leisure. A disadvantage is that it is not easy to control the respondent base; once the questionnaires are sent out, the actual response is dictated by the nature of the sample population. The wrong person may receive a questionnaire. The wrong interpretation may be given to a specific question. Most important is that the actual response level cannot be accurately determined in advance. It is therefore essential to be conservative in planning the sample size for a mail survey.

All four survey mechanisms can be used. Experience indicates that the most cost-efficient approach is to use a limited personal interview process with an open-ended format to develop a final, acceptable questionnaire and survey design and then execute a close-ended telephone survey with a large sample population.

Processing of Survey Results

Once a survey has been completed, it is necessary to process the results. This can be done by hand, but the most efficient method is to use a computer. The results of in-depth personal interviews and focus group interviews need to be converted into data input for computer processing. Mail surveys can be designed to facilitate direct keying of answers; e.g., mark sensing can be used on the form itself, or a "tab" number can be assigned to each answer, enabling the analyst to record the tab number and response alone, without having to examine the specific question. Telephone surveys usually involve the use of on-line screens to input the answers directly.

Once the answers to the questions are converted into data input, the next step is to analyze the results in terms of:

Responses to individual questions

Responses segmented by size, type of respondent, geographic area, etc.

The percentage answering a specific question

Other kinds of segmentation, based on actual responses

It is critically important that the data be analyzed in a totally objective way. This involves the need to examine each question and its answers with respect to defined segments and other patterns which may emerge from the data results. A well-designed questionnaire is critical to the analysis in ensuring a base of data on respondent characteristics and answers that is rich enough for a full evaluation of the key factors influencing answers and the relationships of answers by individual subsegments and classes. This is particularly important in identifying and evaluating similar and different service needs and requirements and in examining customer satisfaction levels.

The Need for Blind, Confidential Surveys

Experience also shows that the service organization can introduce undesirable bias if it fails to recognize a critical factor in the survey process. In essence, customers respond differently to a survey if they have a preconceived or special view of the purpose of that survey. If, for example, they believe that the survey instrument is to be used as a mechanism for raising service prices or changing service response or repair terms, they may bias their responses. They will also be heavily influenced by both internal and environmental conditions of their business and recent experiences. They may, for example, believe that a critical or negative response will lead to improved service, or they may fear that a critical response will lead to a worsening of service (especially if they believe that the survey instrument is being used to compensate the service engineer). Alternatively, they may believe that a positive response will lead to a worsening of service, or to a further improvement in service.

It is important, for the above reasons, that the market survey instrument be masked as much as possible with respect to the initiating service organization. The survey should be carried out on a blind or confidential basis wherever possible. If the service organization must carry out the survey directly and therefore identify itself, it is particularly important that the survey instructions be very precise with respect to the purpose of the survey; the instructions should offer assurances that the survey results will not be given directly, on a one-for-one basis, to the service engineers. Each survey respondent must be guaranteed anonymity, or at least a commitment that specific responses will not be directly fed back and related to his or her own particular service relationships.

This measure of anonymity must also be guaranteed from an operational standpoint. If the service personnel in the field can directly influence a response, the results of the survey cannot be used as a good measurement of customer satisfaction. They may, however, be helpful in determining where to make short-term improvements in service. Since most people dislike criticizing an individual directly, it is very unlikely that survey respondents will be fairly accurate in giving answers if they believe that the service personnel who are supporting them will see the results. In general, unless a customer is extremely dissatisfied, there will be a bias toward making positive statements about service quality and satisfaction levels. This is, of course, a problem which is overcome by using a blind or confidential survey.

Types of Customer Satisfaction Surveys

Several different types of market surveys have been used by service firms to measure service quality and customer satisfaction levels. Larger service organizations have instituted some type of *internally* generated survey that is conducted quarterly, semiannually, or annually; they send a questionnaire to a sample of their customers. Those surveys are highly qualitative and subjective in nature and are conceived and developed in terms of the company's *own view* of the service factors of importance.

A second approach that is sometimes used is the generalized *multiclient* survey. A third approach involves reader responses to *publication-sponsored* surveys. A fourth approach is the *proprietary, customized survey* designed to evaluate specific service issues and performance on a quantitative basis relative to customer requirements and needs and competition; it is conducted by a professional market research organization.

It should be noted that to be fully utilized without bias, each type of survey should be conducted on a blind and confidential basis.

Each type of customer satisfaction survey offers advantages and disadvantages relative to the needs and requirements of service and marketing management. The strengths and weaknesses of each type of survey are described below.

Internal Surveys

Internal surveys of customers to measure service quality and customer satisfaction are often carried out. The primary problem with internally generated surveys is that they tend to introduce significant bias. Extensive market research has clearly demonstrated that if a service organization sends a questionnaire to a particular customer and labels it for return to that organization, the customer will generally respond with a relatively high degree of bias. In essence, respondents represent themselves as either *more negative* or *more positive* than they actually are. Some customers believe that by responding more negatively, they will get better service without increased cost. Others believe that a negative comment will reduce the quality and responsiveness of service; therefore, they respond more positively in the hopes of reinforcing the quality and responsiveness of the service provided.

Another disadvantage is that the measurement techniques tend to be *extremely subjective*. The questions usually are framed to deal only with the service organization's own performance. They rarely measure competitors' performance either absolutely with respect to market needs and requirements or relative to the firm's own performance. Thus the results are usually only comparable with regard to the service organization itself; it is generally not possible to analyze and evaluate performance relative to competitive services available to the end user. In addition, most internally developed surveys fail to deal with alternatives because of the concern that once the alternatives are presented, the customer may opt for them rather than the existing service portfolio. Thus it is extremely difficult to correlate the current levels of customer satisfaction with the effects of alternative service performance to determine what steps should be taken to improve levels of satisfaction without overresponding. Finally, since the surveys are typically directed toward the *current* customer base, the firm cannot measure responses from customers who are dissatisfied and no longer using the firm and potential customers who have elected not to use the firm in the first place.

Multiclient Surveys

Several market research firms provide multiclient survey measures of service quality and customer satisfaction. The primary problem with multiclient surveys of customer satisfaction is that they generally fail to provide precise and accurate evaluations of performance by individual company and product line; the number of responses is not significant enough statistically to provide a high level of confidence in the results. Also, because generic questionnaires are required for a multiclient approach, it is generally not possible to evaluate specific *differences* in operating procedures and practices or organizational structure, as well as product line and market segment variations. Thus it is not possible to obtain unique or specialized insight. For this reason, multiclient surveys fail to provide a basis for *specific* strategic and tactical recommendations for action by an individual sponsoring firm. In addition, the very nature of multiclient surveys gives each of the sponsoring firms the same lead and knowledge rather than a competitive advantage. Finally, multiclient surveys fail to quantify specific customer requirements by market segment and product line and relate them to perceptions of levels of service provided. It is important to recognize that customer requirements *do vary* by segment and product line; while some customers are either satisfied or over-satisfied, another segment of customers, given the *same* levels of service, could be extremely dissatisfied.

In summary, the typical multiclient surveys are difficult to administer and control, since they must deal with the multiclient committee. They are also highly insensitive to strategic competitive differences, and they fail to accurately measure the entire customer base, particularly those customers who are dissatisfied (i.e., they never were or no longer are customers). The survey results are somewhat biased because the approach lacks adequate control by individual firm, market segment, and product line; for example, there is no way to directly evaluate an individual firm's reallocation of resources in order to customize and fine-tune service performance.

Multiclient surveys are, on the other hand, much less expensive than proprietary, or specially commissioned, surveys, with which they compete. Also, they are a valuable means for gaining an understanding of general trends within an existing service portfolio. However, they cannot be used to evaluate the strategic actions of a specific company or to develop new, specialized services to meet emerging or rapidly changing market requirements; only the proprietary surveys are appropriate for these objectives.

Publication-Based Surveys, or "Beauty Contests"

Some service organizations rely extensively on the results of publi-cation-based reader surveys. Essentially, questionnaires are distributed on an uncontrolled basis—they are included in an issue of a given mag-azine. Interested readers then fill out the questionnaire and mail it back to the magazine offices, where the data are processed and the results compiled. The problems arising from such a survey are obvious. In the first place, the results are not randomly controlled or seeded (i.e., there is not a sufficient number of potential respondents by segment); thus the results have relatively low statistical validity when they are analyzed by segment. Secondly, respondents may not be in a position of authority or involved in purchase decisions; therefore, their attitudes may or may not be meaningful relative to the purchase decision or other important aspects of the market. It is also fairly easy to "stuff the ballot box." For example, a very positive or very negative reader could fill out more than one form, or the service organization, interested in certain results, could, by sending in a number of forms, produce more positive results for itself and more negative results for other organizations. Finally, such surveys can, at best, provide only *simplistic* measures of perfor-mance. They fail to deal with the factors which can influence service im-age and performance or provide multiple dimensions which can be re-lated to the allocation of resources.

Proprietary, or Specially Commissioned, Surveys

A fourth approach used in measuring service quality and customer sat-isfaction is the customized survey. Such surveys are usually conducted on a blind or confidential basis by an independent, third-party market research firm for a single client. The primary advantage of proprietary surveys is that they can be specially tailored to evaluate the impact of the specific strategies and tactics of an individual service organization. Also, they provide an in-depth evaluation of service performance by market segment and product line. Most important, such surveys can be used to gain insight into present and emerging market needs and requirements so that a unique strategic direction can be established. These surveys can also be used to evaluate the value in use of service and to develop effective approaches to service pricing. Finally, the surveys can be sta-tistically validated and controlled, with a capability for both random seeding and specialized seeding to provide sufficient representation for each relevant segment, i.e., customers, noncustomers, and ex-cus-tomers. The primary disadvantage of a customized survey is the cost, which is usually two to three times the cost of a multiclient or internal survey.

Which Type of Survey Is Best?

There is, of course, no one type of survey which is "best" for a service organization. Each type has its own advantages, disadvantages, and costs. The internal surveys should be used to measure current levels of customer satisfaction and monitor service performance over time. The multiclient approach can be used to gain an overview of basic trends, but it is very limited in terms of depth or the ability to isolate, identify, and define new opportunities or fine-tune a service organization's strategy. The publication-based surveys have relatively little use, except as a means for alerting firms to general changes, or for publicity and promotion, particularly if a firm is rated as "best." The best approach for developing an overall service strategy is the proprietary survey; this can be used to identify new service opportunities or new aspects of existing service opportunities.

Design Characteristics of Effective Customer Satisfaction Surveys

Survey Capabilities

The above analysis of customer satisfaction surveys identified the key strengths and weaknesses of each approach, including the levels of bias, segmentation, dimensionality, and accuracy which can be obtained. In general, all four approaches can provide some framework or sense of direction for measuring customer satisfaction with service. However, to be most effective and useful, customer satisfaction surveys must be designed to provide, at a minimum, the following capabilities:

1. *Quantitative measurement of the importance of service in the decision to buy.* The survey should provide a quantitative basis for determining the factors of importance, in both a relative and an absolute sense.

2. *Identification and evaluation of the factors utilized by the marketplace to measure and evaluate service performance.* These include, but are not limited to, service response time, service repair time, and technical diagnostic assistance.

3. *Analysis and evaluation of the quantitative service requirements with*

respect to response, repair, delivery, and installation times. These requirements need to be considered as a function of product, market segment, and geographic needs.

4. *Evaluation of perceived performance of various service competitors against market requirements.*

5. *Evaluation of the value in use of service.*

6. *Evaluation of service representatives' performance and capabilities.*

7. *Evaluation of the effects of alternative procedures, policies, and strategies for service delivery.*

8. *Analysis and evaluation of individual service product requirements.* These include, but are not limited to, 24-hour-a-day coverage, 7-day-a-week coverage, remote diagnostic assistance, and the delivery of parts and consumable items.

Structure of Questions

The most important issue to be quantitatively measured is the perception of a service firm's image and performance in relation to both competition and customer requirements. The surveys should be defined in terms which are *meaningful* to the customer and which can be utilized by a specific service organization as a prescription for the reallocation of resources. It is, for example, very trivial to ask such basic questions as whether or not a customer is "very satisfied," "satisfied," or "dissatisfied" with service, since the question assumes that satisfaction can be determined on an absolute rather than relative basis. In addition, differences in the levels of satisfaction cannot be directly related to the performance of competitive service organizations.

It is extremely important to be able to determine the customer's perception of what constitutes excellent, good, or poor service and to be able to then compare the performance of a firm with that of competitors and with the absolute requirements. The use of a linear scale (such as 1 to 5 or 1 to 9) is best for this type of measurement.

Also very important is the need to provide a *quantitative* basis for examining the impact on service of alternative procedures, policies, and allocations of resources. For example, a question such as "What happens when a service engineer arrives on site?" can be extremely useful as an allocation mechanism if one finds that in a significant percentage of cases, the service engineer has to leave and return at a later date because of a lack of parts. Such an analysis can be the basis for a reallocation of inventory levels in order to improve the service engineer's fill rate* and thereby improve overall service responsiveness and employee productivity.

With respect to the four types of customer surveys described above, it is important that questions be designed to:

1. Deal with *customer attitudes* and perceptions, on the basis of *customer terminology and issues*

2. Present the survey as *quantitative and action-oriented*

3. Obtain an objective, quantitative, and comprehensive *survey for all classes* of customers and noncustomers on a *statistically valid* basis

4. Examine existing *call-handling procedures* and *capture actual service response and performance data*, which can be compared with customer satisfaction levels regarding such issues as ETAs missed, callbacks, and excessive downtime in order to develop benchmarks

5. *Provide a framework* for measuring and evaluating *customer satisfaction and service performance by market segment and product line*

6. *Measure and evaluate the value in use of service and pricing alternatives with regard to a clearly defined service portfolio*

7. Provide a *strategic framework for measuring trends* in the levels of customer satisfaction in order to minimize potential dissatisfaction and reasons for switching to or from a specific vendor

The Importance of Continually Measuring Customer Satisfaction and Service Requirements and Needs

Investing in resources to measure—and thus better manage and control—the service image and perception can effect a significant improvement in service productivity, performance, and efficiency. A more complete understanding of service requirements by market segment, geographic area, and product line is gained. The methods for measuring the service image—which include internal surveys, customized confidential surveys, multiclient surveys, and magazine-sponsored sur-

---

*Fill rate refers to the ability of the stock maintained in the service engineer's trunk or kit to meet day-to-day requirements for parts. The fill rate is determined by dividing the total number of times a part is required into the number of times the part is available. A fill rate of 1.0 means that every time a service engineer goes to the trunk or kit for a part, it is there.

veys—are all being used by service organizations. Each approach has both advantages and disadvantages. In general, all the techniques offer an improvement over the "rule of thumb" or "educated guess" approach to measuring service market perceptions which was used in the past by most service managers. Experience has clearly demonstrated that the development of a quantitative understanding of user needs and requirements, service image, and service performance is crucial to improving service operating strategy, profitability, revenue, and market share.

New Ways to Evaluate Service Requirements and Needs through the Use of Single- and Multidimensional Analyses

Service is not just a single parameter. Customers and vendors can often separate service into elements. The problem facing the service executive is to determine which elements are most important to both his or her own customer and competitive vendors, as well as the similarities and differences by customer size, market segment, or other classification criterion. Obviously, the key service elements which can and should be measured through market research are the most critical factors of importance in the decision to buy and use service. For example, I was able to identify, through open-ended interviews, 21 factors which were most *important* to the customer base in the selection and evaluation of equipment maintenance and repair services (see Table 4-5). Other factors, or elements, are also of interest but much less important. These critical factors were then evaluated in general and for specific market segments (Table 4-6). The performance-rating results can be used in different ways—for example, to show differences by market segment (Fig. 4-1) as well as differences between competitors (Table 4-7) with respect to the critical factors of importance.

It is possible to plot the factors of importance on the horizontal (or x) axis and the performance ratings of individual competitors on the vertical (y) axis. Each two-dimensional plot could fall into one of the four quadrants, as shown in Fig. 4-2. If most of the points fall in the upper right quadrant or the lower left quadrant, optimum performance is achieved, and the points in the upper right quadrant are more significant. However, if plotted results fall in the upper left quadrant, this indicates overkill—i.e., too *much* satisfactory performance for a factor of lower importance. Results falling in the lower right quadrant indicate that important factors are not receiving enough attention.

The use of this two-dimensional analysis to compare *competitors'* per-

Table 4-5. Equipment Service Factors of Importance*

Availability of a full range of services
Quality of maintenance service
Cost of maintenance service
Reputation of service organization
Service response time
Speed of equipment repair
Ability of service representative to fix equipment right the first time
Technical skill and ability of service engineer
Availability of software support
Ability to perform self-maintenance
Availability of extended hours of service
Availability of preventive maintenance service
Availability of spare parts
Long-term service commitment
Availability of resident service technician
Availability of site surveys and consultation
Availability of turnkey systems and support
Availability of equipment leasing programs
Ability to service multiple types of equipment
Single point of contact
Proximity of service locations

*Respondents were asked to rate the importance of 21 factors relating to the selection and evaluation of equipment maintenance and repair services.
SOURCE: D. F. Blumberg & Associates studies of service markets.

formance is illustrated in Fig. 4-3. Gaps and weaknesses in the performance of your firm and competing firms (firms A and B) can be identified. This two-dimensional analysis indicates areas in "your firm" where improvements are needed [factor 3 (on-site repair service) and factor 5 (speed of equipment repair)] and where *too much* service is already provided [e.g., factor 10 (national coverage) and factor 11 (national reputation)]. We can also use this analysis to examine the competitive posture of other firms such as competitors A and B and determine *their* strengths and weaknesses. In addition, differences in service needs by market segment or customer size can be tested and evaluated by means of the same two-dimensional format (see Fig. 4-4).

Table 4-6. Factors of Importance in Evaluating Equipment Maintenance and Repair Services*

(Mean Ratings in General and by Market Segment)

Overall rating of importance	Equipment service factors of importance	Market segment			
		Banks	Finan-cial ser-vices	Retail trade	General services
7.7	Availability of a full range of services	7.7	7.7	7.4	7.8
(8.8)	Quality of maintenance service	[8.5]	(8.9)	[8.7]	(8.8)
7.3	Cost of maintenance service	7.2	7.3	7.3	7.3
7.5	Reputation of service organization	7.1	7.7	7.5	7.6
[8.6]	Service response time	[8.5]	△8.6	[8.7]	[8.6]
△8.5	Speed of equipment repair	[8.5]	8.4	[8.7]	8.5
(8.8)	Ability of service representative to fix equipment right the first time	(8.7)	[8.7]	(8.8)	(8.8)
8.4	Technical skill and ability of service engineer	8.1	8.5	△8.4	△8.5
7.1	Availability of software support	7.1	7.2	7.0	7.2
6.7	Ability to perform self-maintenance	6.9	6.5	6.7	6.9
7.1	Availability of extended hours of service	6.9	7.1	7.0	7.4
6.9	Availability of preventive maintenance service	6.9	7.0	6.0	7.4
8.1	Availability of spare parts	8.1	8.0	8.0	8.4
7.2	Long-term service commitment	6.9	7.0	6.8	7.7
6.3	Availability of resident service technician	6.2	6.5	5.8	6.4
5.6	Availability of site surveys and consultation	5.7	6.0	5.0	5.7
5.2	Availability of turnkey systems and support	5.1	5.4	4.7	5.2
4.6	Availability of equipment leasing programs	4.2	5.3	4.6	4.0
6.7	Ability to service multiple types of equipment	6.4	6.7	6.6	6.9
7.1	Single point of contact	7.1	7.3	7.0	7.0
6.9	Proximity of service locations	6.6	7.2	7.3	6.6

*A scale of 1 ("not important") to 9 ("extremely important") was used. A circle signifies the most important factor; a box signifies the second most important factor; and a triangle signifies the third most important factor.

SOURCE: D. F. Blumberg & Associates study of key market segments.

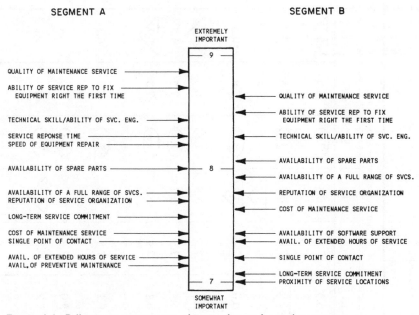

SEGMENT A   SEGMENT B

EXTREMELY
IMPORTANT

9

QUALITY OF MAINTENANCE SERVICE

ABILITY OF SERVICE REP TO FIX
  EQUIPMENT RIGHT THE FIRST TIME   QUALITY OF MAINTENANCE SERVICE

                                                       ABILITY OF SERVICE REP TO FIX
TECHNICAL SKILL/ABILITY OF SVC. ENG.   EQUIPMENT RIGHT THE FIRST TIME

SERVICE REPONSE TIME   TECHNICAL SKILL/ABILITY OF SVC. ENG.
SPEED OF EQUIPMENT REPAIR

                                                       AVAILABILITY OF SPARE PARTS
AVAILABILITY OF SPARE PARTS   8
                                                       AVAILABILITY OF A FULL RANGE OF SVCS.

AVAILABILITY OF A FULL RANGE OF SVCS.   REPUTATION OF SERVICE ORGANIZATION
REPUTATION OF SERVICE ORGANIZATION
                                                       COST OF MAINTENANCE SERVICE
LONG-TERM SERVICE COMMITMENT

COST OF MAINTENANCE SERVICE   AVAILABILITY OF SOFTWARE SUPPORT
SINGLE POINT OF CONTACT   AVAIL. OF EXTENDED HOURS OF SERVICE

AVAIL. OF EXTENDED HOURS OF SERVICE   SINGLE POINT OF CONTACT
AVAIL. OF PREVENTIVE MAINTENANCE
                                                       LONG-TERM SERVICE COMMITMENT
                                           7   PROXIMITY OF SERVICE LOCATIONS

SOMEWHAT
IMPORTANT

Figure 4-1. Differences in importance of service factors, by market segment.

Summary: Service Requirements and Needs

The basic service requirements of customers, both industrial firms and consumers, are in many ways similar to their product requirements. Service, in essence, must fill *some need* described in terms of a form, fit, and function. A need can be as basic as eating and sleeping (i.e., restaurants and hotel service); other needs are services to support financial transactions or health care (banks and hospitals), services to support movement from one location to another (airlines and car rental agencies), and services to support the continuing use of equipment and technology (computer maintenance and equipment repair services).

In examining these requirements, it is critical to differentiate between normal requirements for customer service, which exist in any transaction involving the basic interaction between the firm and its customers, and the delivery and performance of services after the initial sale. This is particularly true where the business transaction involves either consumable or durable goods. In both situations (involving durable and consumable goods), service is strategically critical, but particularly when a durable product is involved, there is a great tendency for management to view service as an *adjunct* or *element* of the product rather than as a stand-alone "product" with its own framework and dimensions.

Table 4-7. Performance Ratings of Competitive Service Organizations* (Mean Ratings Overall and by Competitor)

Overall rating of importance	Equipment service factors of importance	Competitive service organization							
		A	B	C	D	E	F	G	H
7.7	Availability of a full range of services	5.7	6.5	7.6	6.8	7.9	6.6	5.5	6.8
8.8	Quality of maintenance service	6.1	6.0	7.6	6.7	8.0	6.8	6.9	6.1
7.3	Cost of maintenance service	6.2	5.8	6.3	5.2	6.2	6.4	5.8	6.6
7.5	Reputation of service organization	5.7	6.0	7.4	5.4	8.1	6.8	6.3	6.3
8.6	Service response time	6.2	5.5	7.5	5.8	7.8	6.9	5.4	5.7
8.5	Speed of equipment repair	5.2	5.4	7.5	5.7	7.7	7.2	5.3	5.4
8.8	Ability of service representative to fix equipment right the first time	5.8	6.1	7.4	6.5	7.8	7.3	5.1	5.4
8.4	Technical skill and ability of service engineer	5.9	6.1	7.3	6.0	7.8	7.7	6.1	5.9
7.1	Availability of software support	6.5	5.0	7.4	5.0	7.6	7.0	6.4	3.8
6.7	Ability to perform self-maintenance	5.9	5.2	6.8	4.0	7.1	6.2	5.1	4.7

Factor	Importance								
Availability of extended hours of service	7.1	5.9	6.0	7.4	8.1 (circle)	6.0	7.9	6.0	5.0 (triangle)
Availability of preventive maintenance service	6.9	5.0	5.1	5.9	7.4 (circle)	3.3 (triangle)	7.4	6.1	5.3
Availability of spare parts	8.1	5.6	6.4	7.8 (circle)	7.8 (circle)	4.8 (triangle)	7.4	5.9	6.1
Long-term service commitment	7.2	6.3	5.2 (triangle)	7.4	8.1 (circle)	5.8	7.9	6.6	5.9
Availability of resident service technician	6.3	5.8	4.4 (triangle)	6.6	7.5 (circle)	6.3	6.6	5.3	4.8
Availability of site surveys and consultation	5.6	5.3	4.3 (triangle)	7.3	7.4 (circle)	6.2	7.2	5.0	5.9
Availability of turnkey systems and support	5.2	6.5	5.3	7.7 (circle)	6.8	4.8 (triangle)	6.6	5.6	6.4
Availability of equipment leasing programs	4.6	6.7	5.5 (triangle)	8.3 (circle)	7.1	6.7	7.0	5.5 (triangle)	6.0
Ability to service multiple types of equipment	6.7	6.4	6.0	7.9 (circle)	6.8	6.0	6.7	5.7 (triangle)	6.7
Single point of contact	7.1	6.9	5.0 (triangle)	7.2	7.7 (circle)	7.5	7.3	5.4	6.1
Proximity of service locations	6.9	5.9 (triangle)	5.9 (triangle)	7.3	7.9 (circle)	6.0	7.5	6.0	7.1

*A scale of 1 ("not important" or "poor performance") to 9 ("extremely important" or "excellent performance") was used. In the first column, a circle signifies the most important factor; a box signifies the second most important factor; and a triangle signifies the third most important factor. In the lettered columns, a circle indicates the highest performance, and a triangle indicates the lowest performance.

SOURCE: D. F. Blumberg & Associates study of performance of competitive service organizations.

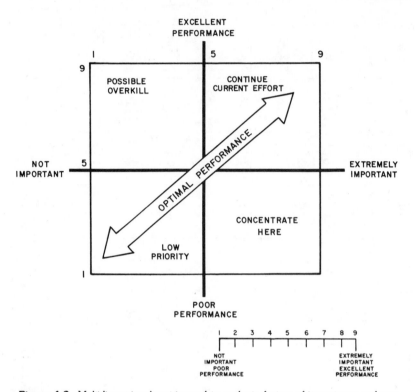

Figure 4-2. Multidimensional matrix used to evaluate factors of importance and performance ratings.

Much has been said about the critical importance of quality in both a product and service, but one must recognize that a customer perceives a difference between the product and service, particularly as the product or service becomes more accepted and more mature. In substance, the customer recognizes that in any transaction there will be some failure to perform: the service establishment will become busy at the time when the customer wishes to use its facilities, or the product may fail at the time when the customer needs to use it. It is this particular situation that creates the true strategic value of service. Service quality is rated on the basis of a broad variety of perceptions (drawn from experience, merchandising, peer recommendations, etc.) about the ability of the service organization to provide service when it is needed. A successful service organization recognizes that the real requirements for service are related to future performance. Since service is intangible, customers must make their purchase decisions generally before they have a chance to touch and observe what they are purchasing. Their service requirements are based much more on perceptions of reality than on reality itself.

This is not to suggest that an effective service organization can simply

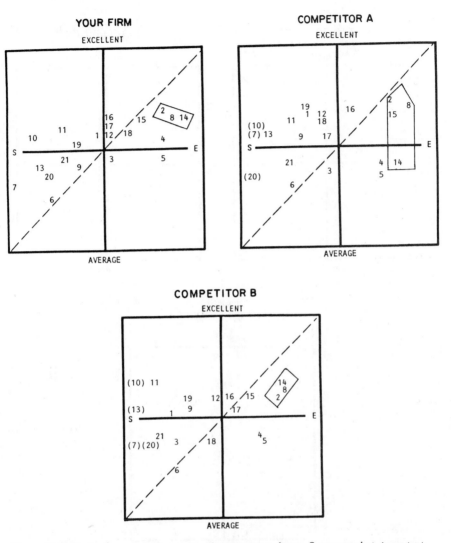

Figure 4-3. Evaluation of performance of competitive firms. S = somewhat important; E = extremely important; dashed line = ideal profile. Service selection factors: 1 = availability of a full range of services; 2 = quality of service; 3 = ability to provide on-site repair service; 4 = service response time; 5 = speed of equipment repair; 6 = cost of service; 7 = size of service organization; 8 = technical skill and ability of service technician; 9 = depot repair capability; 10 = national coverage; 11 = national reputation; 12 = local reputation; 13 = availability of a service contract; 14 = parts supply; 15 = performance guarantee; 16 = past experience with product manufacturer; 17 = past experience with service provider; 18 = availability of training; 19 = application engineering capability; 20 = project management capability; 21 = proximity of service locations.

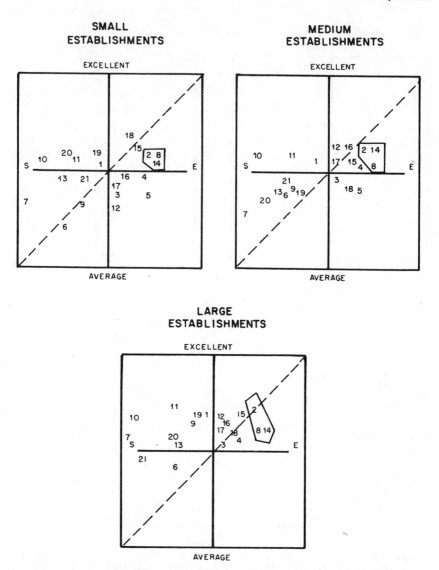

Figure 4-4. Differences in service needs by customer type or market segment. S = somewhat important; E = extremely important; dashed line = ideal profile. Service selection factors: 1 = availability of a full range of services; 2 = quality of service; 3 = ability to provide on-site repair service; 4 = service response time; 5 = speed of equipment repair; 6 = cost of service; 7 = size of service organization; 8 = technical skill and ability of service technician; 9 = depot repair capability; 10 = national coverage; 11 = national reputation; 12 = local reputation; 13 = availability of a service contract; 14 = parts supply; 15 = performance guarantee; 16 = past experience with product manufacturer; 17 = past experience with service provider; 18 = availability of training; 19 = application engineering capability; 20 = project management capability; 21 = proximity of service locations.

ignore performance and concentrate on manipulating and controlling perceptions. The real requirements for service must be measured, understood, and controlled in terms of both the customer's perceptions and realities. These perceptions primarily concern critical time issues— the length of time to wait for the service technician, or the length of time for the performance of service, or both. Time criticality tends to be a universal factor—one that is relevant to all types of services (for example, waiting time in a restaurant, on-time performance of an airline, and the time it takes a salesclerk to ring up a sale). Time is the *one factor* which tends to differentiate a product from service. It is customers' perceptions of performance at a future time which constitute the primary differentiating mechanism in service.

5
Developing and Planning the Service Organization

The Service Plan

Once we have developed a market focus and a strategy defining the services to be offered, we can begin to develop and implement the service plan. The critical first step is to answer these questions:

Who are the targeted customers for the service(s)?

What are their needs and requirements, in terms of service time and related performance parameters?

How often do the service demands occur for the targeted customer base?

How much are these customers willing to pay?

These questions need to be asked and answered for both products and services. For services, the customer base can be determined directly. All individual consumers, industrial and commercial firms, and government agencies and organizations require and need a broad variety of services. For products, the service-related opportunities are defined by looking at the customers for the products and determining their service needs both directly related to the products and indirectly related to the operating environment in which the products are found, used, or applied. Some of these product-driven services may be tied directly to the tangible product, as in the case of product warranties and liability, product training, product modification and upgrades, and product maintenance and repair. Other services may be related to the larger product or technology base of the customer.

It is important in developing this strategic identification of the customer and the service needs to make use of market survey techniques (see Chap. 4) and to examine the service needs objectively and logically. Service requirements and needs may often be hidden by past practices or "conventional wisdom." The best opportunities exist for new services which focus on

- Unmet existing requirements
- More cost-effective approaches to existing service requirements
- The creation of new service-related needs

There are numerous examples of service-related businesses driven by such opportunities.

Fast-food restaurants, driven by the unmet need for standardized-quality food provided quickly and inexpensively

Same- and next-day delivery services, driven by unmet requirements for rapid package transportation

Third-party maintenance services for computers and other high-technology repair services, driven by the need for more cost-effective support

The service plan should provide the framework in which the service requirements can be optimally met. The plan must specify:

- The portfolio of services which will be supplied
- The service delivery mechanisms and information to be used
- The personnel and logistics required to provide the services
- The management structure and systems for coordinating, controlling, and delivering the services
- The price of the services to achieve optimum balance with respect to the target customers' willingness to pay
- The marketing and sales approach to penetrate the customer base

In addition, if the services are developed in the framework of an existing market, the plan needs to identify the competitive service alternatives from the customers' perspective and describe the key methods to penetrate the market.

Determining Service Staff and Support Levels

Because of the labor-intensive nature of service, staffing is generally one of the most important service plan elements to be developed. Determining the size of the service organization is usually the key to examining the economic viability of the service opportunity and the dimensions of the infrastructure and logistics support required.

Determining the Direct Service Staff Level

The first step in planning the direct service force is to convert the proposed or actual service portfolio into the service requirement per customer. This is usually computed by establishing the service period (in terms of hours per day, days per week, etc.) and the mean time between service demands. The overall service requirement is then determined by multiplying the individual-customer requirement by the number of customers in the targeted customer base. Actual service performance time will be affected by the time required to prepare for and initiate the service (response time) and the actual service task completion time. Response time will be affected by the need to travel from a service center to a customer's location and by the need to assemble service resources (such as parts). Service completion time will be affected by the skill level and training of the service staff; the availability of materials, parts, or consumable items required to provide the service; and infrastructure support. The response time and completion time can then be used to determine the overall service completion rate.

The key to the final computation of the staff level is to recognize that from the customer's viewpoint, total service performance time will also be affected by the waiting time required before a service assignment can be initiated. Since, for service to be cost-effective, there must be a close balance between the service requirement of the customer and the service capability of the organization, the customer generally must wait in line for service to be provided. The length of this waiting line, or service queue, will be affected by both the service completion rate and the availability or utilization of service personnel. In effect, the ratio between service time available and service personnel utilized will directly affect the waiting time. If service personnel are available or not busy with another customer, they can respond to this customer's needs. Thus there is a relationship between utilization of service personnel and service response time (as viewed by the customer). This relationship is not usually linear; it is, in fact, S-shaped, as shown in Fig. 5-1, for a typical service situation. The dimensions and position of the curve relating response

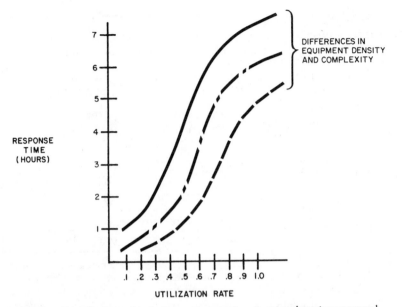

Figure 5-1. Typical relationship between response time target and service personnel utilization rate. Based on empirically derived research in high-tech equipment markets.

time to productivity or utilization rate will, of course, change from situation to situation, but in general, the more rapid the response required by the customer, the lower the direct utilization of the service staff and direct productivity. The curve is S-shaped because it is easier to provide service for a larger group of customers who are willing to wait a longer period of time than to serve the same group demanding rapid response. The more rapid the response desired, the greater the number of service people who must be positioned in advance, waiting for a customer to arrive or call for service.

An analytical model of waiting time for service, called *queuing theory,* * can be used to compute the S-shaped service response–utilization relationships for specific situations. However, the curves shown in Fig. 5-1 provide a reasonable approximation of such relationships, particularly for high-tech equipment, on the basis of extensive empirical research.

Given these relationships, it is then possible to determine the service staff level that will generally achieve a specific service performance time target. The general model calculations shown in Fig. 5-2 can be used to determine the direct service staff level. For example, assume that a de-

---

*Many texts are available on queuing theory and queuing models. (See the Bibliography.)

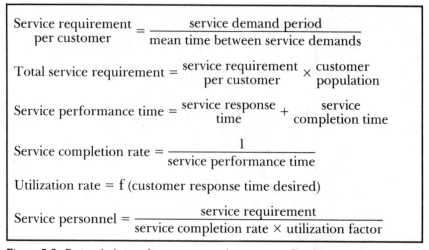

$$\frac{\text{Service requirement}}{\text{per customer}} = \frac{\text{service demand period}}{\text{mean time between service demands}}$$

$$\text{Total service requirement} = \frac{\text{service requirement}}{\text{per customer}} \times \frac{\text{customer}}{\text{population}}$$

$$\text{Service performance time} = \frac{\text{service response}}{\text{time}} + \frac{\text{service}}{\text{completion time}}$$

$$\text{Service completion rate} = \frac{1}{\text{service performance time}}$$

$$\text{Utilization rate} = f \text{ (customer response time desired)}$$

$$\text{Service personnel} = \frac{\text{service requirement}}{\text{service completion rate} \times \text{utilization factor}}$$

Figure 5-2. Basic calculation of service personnel requirement. The f means a function of desired customer response time as expressed in the derived performance curves in Fig. 5-1.

mand for service occurs approximately once every 80 days and that the service demand period is from 9 a.m. to 5 p.m. (8 hours per day). Further, assume that the customer population is 1000, that 1 hour is required to respond (or prepare to accomplish the service task), and that 1 hour is required to complete the service task. We need only to establish the service response time target (say 4.5 hours) for the typical customer. The response target can then be converted into a utilization or efficiency rate (from the typical S-shaped curve in Fig. 5-1) which is used to determine the direct service force level required. Figure 5-3 shows the calculations used in this example to determine the direct service staff required to support a targeted customer population requiring a specific service response. In this solution, the answer is 4.46 service personnel, or approximately 5 people.

These calculations are, of course, merely illustrative; they show the approach which can be used in planning the direct service staff. The most complex task is to determine the S-curve parameters. This can be done by using pragmatic experience and field tests or by using queuing models.

Determining the Support Staff Level

Once the direct service staff level is determined, it is then possible to develop plans for the support staff, including management and supervisory personnel. The number of management and supervisory personnel can be determined by establishing the organizational and opera-

Assume:

Service demand period = 8 hours per day, 5 days per week

Mean time between service demands = 80 days = 640 hours

Customer population = 1000

Specific service response time = 1 hour

Specific service completion time = 1 hour

Customer service response time target = 4.5 hours

Then:

Service requirement per day $= \dfrac{8}{640} \times 1000 = 12.5$

Service completion rate per service person $= \dfrac{1}{0.125 + 0.125}$

$$= \dfrac{1}{0.25} = 4 \text{ per day}$$

Utilization rate (from the middle curve in Fig. 5-1) = 0.7

Direct service personnel requirement $= \dfrac{12.5}{4 \times 0.7} = 4.465 \approx 5$

Figure 5-3. Example of calculation of service staff requirement. *Customer service response time target*: the overall waiting time for an individual customer between the time the service is originally requested and the time the service is completed.

tional structures and the span-of-control ratios. Experience suggests that the level of organizational control (centralized, regional, or decentralized) will affect both the size and the dimensions of the service management organization, with fewer staff required in a centralized organization than in a regional or decentralized one. On the other hand, the more flexible and customized the services to be provided, the greater the need for local management and supervision. Computerization and the use of communications and coordination networks and related technology will also affect the ability to efficiently manage and control the service organization. These topics will be discussed in more detail in Chaps. 8 and 9. A good rule of thumb is that the span of control at the local service level should not exceed 10 to 15 direct service staff, and control at the general management level should not exceed 6 to 8. Thus the initial sizing of the direct service staff can be used to develop estimates of supervisory and management staff.

Support staff responsibilities include:

Technical support

Logistics control, including the coordination of materials

Training

Customer service, including service call handling

Financial and administrative control

Marketing and sales

These responsibilities will vary greatly from one service business to another. However, a typical ratio is approximately 1 support staff member for every 1.5 direct service personnel. Thus a typical service organization would have a total staff of 2.5 personnel (excluding management and supervisory personnel) for every direct service position required.

Planning for Logistics and Infrastructure Support

In addition to staff, a service organization must have the appropriate facilities, infrastructure, and logistics support. Here again, the requirements will vary from one service business to another. Restaurants require a different mix and investment level than retail stores, banks, or equipment maintenance services. In general, support technology for service coordination, delivery, and control provides a high return on investment, with the payback as short as 1 to 2 years.

In most service organizations, it is necessary to control logistics and materials centrally and dynamically. The full coordination of the materials and parts supply cycle will normally require control by individual stockkeeping unit, down to and including the point of use. Recording the parts, materials, and consumables used to complete a service task is critical to controlling inventory and maximizing inventory turnover and return on investment.

Establishing Material Requirements and Stock Fill Rates

Material requirements are normally developed by examining the stock needs of each type of service request and acquiring and allocating these supplies, equipment items, etc., to satisfy customer requirements on the basis of anticipated demands. Stocking goals need to be established in terms of a fill rate: the ratio determined by dividing the number of times stock is available to fill customer service requirements by the total number of customer requests.* To achieve a high fill rate, a high investment in stock is required. Just as in the case of determining a staff level, logistics investment can be set by establishing customers' service time requirements and willingness to pay and determining the stock levels to meet these needs. A fill rate of 95 percent or better is required to achieve a high level of customer satisfaction. Thus a retail store catering to a broad array of customers or special interests will require a larger inventory than a store with a narrower focus.

Inventory pipeline control can also be affected by the logistics system and structure. Using central warehouses or depots to resupply local stocking points can be much more efficient in terms of inventory turnover and return on investment than decentralizing stock levels and control. In service organizations with many local branches or geographically decentralized field service operations, it is essential to manage the full inventory pipeline, from central and regional stocks to local stocks. This is accomplished through the coordinated recoding of stock use, forecasts of demand, and the establishment of maximum and minimum stock levels by location to facilitate reordering.

Managing Returns

In some service organizations, there is an important return cycle in logistics support. For example, in equipment maintenance and repair services, parts, subassemblies, and whole units are turned in as part of the process of servicing equipment. Since items worth approximately 60 to 80 percent of the total value of the inventory could be turned in for some type of technology in any one year, the return cycle also must be managed and controlled. Refurbishment and repair of these returned items make it possible for the service organization to efficiently use them to refill the inventory pipeline.

Human Resources

Once the appropriate levels for both the direct service staff and the support staff have been defined, it is then important to develop and implement the full array of actions needed to manage the human resources. Since service is generally provided by the direct service staff and requests for service and complaints about service are handled by both cus-

---

*For example, if parts are required by a service engineer 30 times in order to perform repairs and on 25 occasions the parts are available in the service engineer's trunk or kit, the fill rate is 25 ÷ 30, or 0.833. A higher fill rate reduces repair time and the number of "broken" calls due to lack of parts. It also increases inventory investment.

tomer service and service management personnel, it should be quite clear that the selection, acquisition, development, training, and motivation of the staff are critical in terms of managing both the actual service delivery and the customers' perceptions.

Identifying and Defining the Service Staff Positions

The first step in managing human resources is to clearly define the individual service positions in terms of roles and responsibilities, work assignment, and prerequisites for employment (education and training, experience, etc.). The description of each position should clearly define the minimum or basic skill and education levels. Specific reference should be made to the behavioral and social skills which will be required in the position.

Attracting and Acquiring Individuals for the Service Staff

A service staff can be developed both from within the organization and through external acquisition. Since many service skills can be acquired through on-the-job training, advertisements for positions should stress the basic skills and capabilities required rather than very high levels of education and experience.

Addressing Special Issues in Acquiring Service Managers and Executives

Special attention needs to be paid to the recruitment and acquisition of experienced service managers and executives. In general, management and executive personnel who were not trained in a service environment often lack an orientation toward the customer and an understanding of service needs and requirements. It is, therefore, desirable to try to obtain managers and executives who have at least a small amount of experience interacting with customers and service-related staff in a service environment.

Providing Training for Staff Development

Crucial to the successful management of human resources in a service organization is training in both specific and general service-related skills and disciplines. Courses should be developed in both customer awareness and the particular service strategy and direction of the organization. It is critical that all service personnel, including the direct service staff and the support staff, fully understand the service mission of the organization and the organizational and operational structures with respect to service management and delivery. A specific training program should be developed for the personnel who handle calls from customers, for these calls involve the most critical interaction with customers. Training sessions can make use of a variety of tools and techniques, including:

Classroom instruction

Videotapes and other personnel training aids

Quality circles or groups and rap sessions focusing on improving customer satisfaction levels

On-the-job training

Programs to improve service staff sensitivity concerning customer service levels and customer satisfaction should be fully employed. Printing monthly or quarterly newsletters on service issues and conducting quarterly and annual surveys to evaluate current levels of service performance and customer satisfaction are two methods often used to improve service awareness.

Reports that evaluate customers' satisfaction with customer service and after-sales service should be developed by both service operating function and geographic area. This type of reporting can be used to heighten awareness of the critical values of customer satisfaction with service, as well as to establish competitive goals for peer groups to maximize customer satisfaction levels.

Establishing Compensation Levels

Compensation levels should, of course, be established for each staff position as a function of experience, education, skills, level of responsibility, and degree of interaction with customers. A combination of job skills assessment, minimum educational and experience requirements, and responsibility assessment should be used to establish the minimum and maximum salaries for each position.

Compensation and performance reviews should be carried out on an annual basis for all staff, as well as on a semiannual basis for critical customer service personnel.

Special bonuses for exceeding service goals should also be established. They can be an incentive to employees, motivating them to maximize customer satisfaction levels and to be responsive, on a timely basis, to customer needs and requirements. Independent customer satisfaction surveys (discussed in Chap. 4) can be used to provide an objective evaluation of service performance.

Warranty Services

Product or service sales are usually made under some type of warranty, or guarantee of quality and performance. Typical warranty periods regarding product and service failure range from 1 month to 1 year. Many product manufacturers are increasing the time for warranty coverage to further highlight their commitment to service. The services provided to cover either product failure or lack of service performance should be based upon a carefully developed plan and specific operational practices and procedures.

The first step in establishing a warranty program is to clearly define the period of time the product or service is covered. The extent of coverage should be based upon the inherent quality or reliability of the product or service, as well as its failure rate. Factors to consider are the actual mean time between failures and/or the mean time between service calls, competitive practices, and customers' willingness to pay for service. It is generally recommended that a warranty be provided for a minimum of 6 months to 1 year. This suggests to the customer a strong commitment to both quality and service. In addition, the customer relies on the organization for service and support over a period that is long enough for establishing a close relationship.

The services provided under the warranty to correct problems should be performed on the basis of a warranty service budget, which is established by the service organization and the product or primary service business unit through objective negotiation. Estimates of service calls based on experience or anticipated service demand rates can be used to calculate the service force required to support the warranty. The calculation involves essentially the same steps that were used to estimate the service staff level. Multiplying the service personnel needed to meet the warranty requirements by the fully loaded cost of a service person gives a dollar amount that can then be used to establish a budget for the warranty services to be rendered. The warranty price should be added to the standard product or service price, since the warranty is an additional cost item.

Under the strategic service approach, a transfer price should be established between the product manufacturer or the basic service organization and the service support organization to cover the warranty. In this way, the manufacturer's or service organization's full cost of service delivery is covered under the warranty. Warranty services are treated in the same way as the services provided for the customer directly after the warranty period. The product manufacturer or service organization will, therefore, achieve a profit or a loss depending upon its capability to serve and its ability to both meet the service performance goals established by the warranty and provide service after the warranty period. Careful and accurate reports on product or service failures make it possible to determine, within close limits, the actual costs of warranty and continuing service. The initial negotiated agreement between the product manufacturer or service organization and the service support organization should then be reevaluated to create a profit margin for the manufacturer or service organization based on a discount, as opposed to the normal margins it achieves from after-warranty services. This discount should reflect the sales and administrative costs and profit margins of the product manufacturer or service organization for its generation of the tie-in business. The transfer price that is set for warranty support should allow the service support organization to make a reasonable profit on the warranty business, assuming that it is efficient in the delivery of that service; the transfer price should be calculated by determining the competitive market price for equivalent service performance.

An important element of the warranty program is the need to establish procedures for tracking and controlling warranty services, as opposed to after-warranty services. This can be accomplished by a full service management system which collects data on all service calls (both under the warranty and after the warranty period), including costs and performance levels.

6
Marketing Service

The growing recognition of the opportunity to achieve high revenues and profits from services run as a line of business has been accompanied by a greater focus on marketing service. Historically, in industries involved in the manufacture of tangible products, service was viewed as an add-on. The costs of delivery, installation, and warranty services were usually embedded in the price of the product. Marketing service was not, in that framework, important. Contracts for maintenance service on a time-and-materials basis were generated almost automatically or through the unofficial and informal efforts of the local sales or service personnel in the field. Most managers tended to think about service as an automatic "annuity."

Pricing services was normally based on some simplistic approach, similar to pricing products, involving estimated costs plus a markup. Some organizations provided an incentive, such as a bonus or commission, for the sales force or service force to encourage the generation of additional service revenues. In those cases, service prices were also marked up to reflect the incentives. However, these mechanisms were often viewed tactically rather than as an integral part of the general strategic thrust toward developing service as a line of business. In fact, in many cases, the price of service was adjusted downward in an attempt to initially sell the tangible products.

The growing recognition of the revenue and profit potential from service as a separate business, the trend toward the provision of service and maintenance, and growing competition for the service dollar have all created the need for a specific marketing strategy for service operations. The most effective service marketing plan involves the following tasks:

1. Characterize explicitly the services to be offered, and *establish* the content of a *service portfolio*.
2. Develop and articulate the service portfolio on the basis of an explicit consideration of the *customers' requirements and willingness to pay*, determined from market research.
3. *Merchandise and package* the service portfolio.
4. *Sell* the services offered both *directly and indirectly*.

Characterizing the Service Portfolio Offered

The service portfolio must be initially described in terms of both *direct performance* and *guarantees of response and performance* in the event of future service needs. The portfolio must satisfy both *perceived* and *actual* requirements of the customer base. A typical array of services is shown in Table 6-1. This comparison indicates that there are very real differences between the actual *delivery or performance* of a service and the *future perceived return*. In addition to the basic services, a service portfolio can contain other support elements, such as the delivery of

Table 6-1. Basic Services

Basic service	Actual delivery (the service actually provided for the customer)	Future perceived return (what the customer expects to occur in the future)
Installation	Equipment installed at customer site within the time specified	Functions of equipment operational within time specified
Warranty	Service, repair, and correction of initial problems occurring after installation	No problems of a significant nature after installation, for the warranty period
Maintenance and repairs Software Hardware	Arrival on site within reasonable time, and completion of repair	Insurance that failure of equipment will not cause disruption in operations or use
Moves, additions, and changes	Correction, upgrading, or modification of equipment and/or software	New or changing requirements satisfied on a timely basis without disruptions

SOURCE: In-depth customer survey and interviews.

Table 6-2. Support Services

Service item	Characteristics
Training	Provision of training for operators and users
Documentation	User, systems, and support documentation
Software support	Provision for finding software and/or modifying software to meet specific customer needs
Parts and supplies	Delivery of parts and/or supplies upon order
Depot repair or rehabilitation	Rehab and/or repair at local, regional, or central depot (i.e., not on site)

parts and/or supplies, software support, and training (see Table 6-2). The service portfolio must be defined on a *multidimensional* basis; there is a need to include *both* the element of performance and the element of response and coverage time (e.g., time targets for installation, maintenance, and repairs) for both basic and support services (Fig. 6-1). In summary, the service portfolio needs to be defined and described in terms of the mix of elements which can be offered by the service organization to various market segments and customer bases.

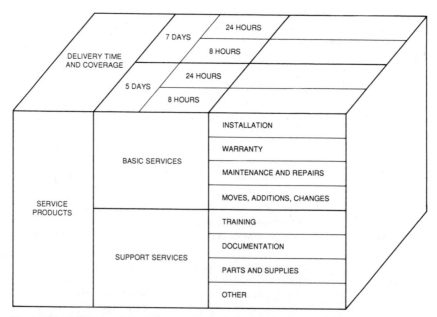

Figure 6-1. A full service portfolio showing the key dimensions: time-of-day and day-of-week coverage, and basic and support services.

Marketing Services: Key Factors and Focus

The sale of a service has been a problem facing a very large number of organizations since the dawn of commercial enterprise. Numerous services, ranging from legal and accounting services to advertising and physical distribution, are merchandised, packaged, and sold every day. In developing a marketing plan for service, it is important to recognize that service is an intangible; therefore, the *perception* of the quality and *value in use* of service is as *important* as the actual delivery of services. For example, a lawyer's or doctor's services are often chosen not because of actual performance or price but because of the customer's perception of the improvement in health, position, or circumstances which will result *in the future* from the use of the services today. Thus we can see that services are generally characterized by a *future* element—the potential for change, reduction in risk, or improvement in satisfaction. Therefore, the definition of a service "product" must consider two critical elements:

1. The *actual characterization of service delivery* (i.e., what is to be provided)
2. *Future return to the customer* as a result of utilizing the service

For example, in the case of repair services at a local gas station, one is paying for both the actual performance of service (such as lubrication or changing spark plugs) and a reduction in the risk of a future breakdown. In the case of accounting services, one is paying for both a professional review of the books and a reduction in the risk of being unable to pass an Internal Revenue Service audit.

It is essential that the service organization, in developing its service portfolio mix, understand the characteristics of importance *to the customer* with respect to the future perceived value of the services. Focusing on only the actual delivery of services is not sufficient. For both customer service and field service, the primary elements are both the initial service, including service response (such as physical delivery within a given time frame), and the future value of the service from the *customer's perspective*, such as the ability to use the delivered product.

Meeting Customer Needs and Requirements

As discussed in Chap. 2, a major factor influencing the general shape of the service business strategy and marketing approach is the particular customer needs and requirements which exist in the targeted market segments. I have already pointed out (in Chap. 3) that a customer places the highest emphasis on service response and repair *times*. I showed that there is a high correlation between the ability to deliver service in a given or desired *time frame* and *satisfaction* with service. On the other hand, I pointed out that the satisfaction levels tend to have a step pattern. That is, customer satisfaction levels drop substantially when time objectives or requirements are *not met*. For each type of product (e.g., mainframes, minicomputers, microprocessors, personal computers, peripherals, automatic teller machines, and point-of-sale equipment) in each specific market segment (e.g., process manufacturing, discrete manufacturing, banking, and retail trade), the customer has reasonably well-defined requirements as to acceptable service response and repair times, installation times, etc. The *type of product*, the *market segment*, and the *use of the equipment* all tend to dictate the levels of service performance and the time frame of response which are necessary to achieve given levels of customer satisfaction.

It is particularly important to recognize and measure (through market research) both the *existence* of these well-defined time requirements and the *nonlinear*, or *step*, pattern which describes customer satisfaction. I have shown that service quality is most often evaluated by the customer at times when the service organization *fails to perform*. Thus it is not so much the *actual* performance but the ability to avoid *critical failures in targeted time frames*, on the average, which tends to most heavily influence customer satisfaction levels. I have also shown that customers' perceptions of service quality can also be influenced, either positively or negatively, by *peer comments* and other *secondary sources*.

On the other hand, customers are generally insensitive to the provision of service at a level which is *significantly more rapid* than they require. There is, therefore, an *equal penalty* (i.e., an increase in cost and, consequently, a reduction in profit margins) associated with providing *too much* service. A service organization needs to accurately measure customer needs and requirements for service, particularly with regard to time parameters, and then ensure that service is provided to *just meet* those time objectives. Market segments which have a high-density installed base *and* critical response and repair time requirements are the markets which could be the most profitable. This is especially true if value-in-use pricing, previously explained, is utilized. The prices for the focused service portfolio will depend on the product-service cross elasticity discussed in Chap. 3. The full application of alternative approaches to pricing is covered in Chap. 7.

Once the service requirements and needs of specific market segments are fully identified, it is important to understand the role of perception in setting prices for service. In a product business, two dimensions normally are used (from the marketing perspective) to define the product:

The form, fit, and function of the product

The label

The form, fit, and function describe what the product is, what it does, and how it is used. The label provides the customer with a perceived mark of quality and satisfaction level. Typically, a well-known, quality label (such as Kodak, IBM, or Ford) can increase the price 10 to 100 percent over the prices of competitive products because of the added value which the perception provides. The label is merchandised and marketed, and when attached to the product, it adds value. An IBM product, for example, may command a price that is 10 to 25 percent higher than the prices of competitive products.

For a service, two dimensions *also* exist:

The form, fit, and function of the service (i.e., what it is, what it does, and how it is used)

The perception (i.e., the current view of future service performance as a label)

Just as in the product example, the perception of service (the "label") can add value. The major difference, however, is that in service, perceptions can have a much greater impact on value added (anywhere from 10 to 1000 percent or more). For example, a surgeon or attorney known for quality service performance can *often* command two to three times the price of competing professionals. Service perceptions can add much greater value to service price than product perceptions add to product price (see Table 6-3). Thus service pricing not only is much more sophisticated but also requires a full knowledge of market perceptions of the quality of the vendor's delivered service.

Merchandising and Packaging the Service Portfolio

With a specific view of customer needs and requirements in the targeted market segments established, the next step in developing and implementing an effective service marketing strategy is to properly merchandise and package the service portfolio. This must be done in the context of customer perceptions and values and in a form which

Table 6-3. Differences between Marketing Products and Marketing Service

Marketing dimensions	Products	Services
Form, fit, function	What it is What it does How it is used	What it is What it does How it is used
Perception	Label	Current view of future performance
Value-added potential of perception		
	10–100% price variation	10–1000% price variation

can be easily perceived by the individual targeted market segments. Merchandising and packaging constitute an obvious step in developing a strategy for a product business; it is often overlooked in service marketing because of the belief that intangibles such as service cannot be packaged or merchandised. Service executives, particularly service marketing managers, must focus as specifically as possible on the needs of individual service markets and especially on the unique service requirements. A good example is the service needs of *vertical market segments*, such as hospitals, hotels, banks, retail stores, brokerage organizations, and manufacturing firms. The service needs of those vertical market segments differ greatly. For example, hospitals operate around the clock, 7 days a week, whereas a bank operates 5 days a week, 8 hours a day. The service response time requirements also differ. A hospital or bank needs service more rapidly than does a retail establishment. A specific focus on the service needs and requirements of individual market segments through the creation of a specialized service portfolio is the starting point in efficiently merchandising and packaging services.

There are a variety of mechanisms for packaging and merchandising services, including, but not limited to:

- Brochures
- Advertising
- Participation in trade shows and trade associations
- Direct mail
- Service follow-up mailers

Specific mechanisms for merchandising and packaging services are listed in Table 6-4. Additional important methods of service merchandising include word-of-mouth, or reference, selling. Because of the intangible and primarily perceived nature of the service portfolio, a positive reference from a satisfied customer carries great weight for a potential buyer. References can be directly solicited or determined through confidential mailings and surveys. Satisfied service customers' testimony and comments can generate an extremely powerful positive perception. Positive reference selling can also be achieved through advertising the experiences and recommendations of satisfied customers. Market segment awareness and perception of service quality can also be influenced through articles in trade publications and professional jour-

Table 6-4. Service Merchandising and Packaging Mechanisms

Mechanism	Application
Newsletter	Provides continuing awareness of service activity for existing customer base
Service follow-up mailer	Sent after service or installation call to determine satisfaction; improves perception of commitment to service
Brochure	Tends to "productize" service; articulates the delivery; creates perceptions of "existence"
Service management system (call handling and dispatch, national 800 number, etc.)	Provides perceived mechanism for service management and control; demonstrates mechanism for ensuring performance
Advertising	Display ad in trade magazines and newspapers: promotes awareness of service availability and increases perception of commitment
	Radio or TV ad: useful in opening up or expanding regional markets, in conjunction with other merchandising mechanisms
Direct mail	Focuses attention on particular market segments; useful in conjunction with brochure
Trade show booth and exhibition	Increases perception of commitment to service particularly if primary focus is on service performance and delivery

nals, speeches, etc. Services can be merchandised and packaged through formal and direct mechanisms as well as informal and indirect methods.

Selling Services

The final step in developing and implementing an effective service marketing strategy is the management of the continuing process of sales, distribution, and contract commitments. For field service and logistics support services, this can be accomplished directly by an assigned sales force or indirectly by sales representatives or a collateral sales force (such as the product sales personnel).

Historically, field service was sold through indirect or collateral sales organizations. However, as service is becoming established as a separate line of business with specific revenue and profit margin objectives, service organizations are increasingly developing their own direct sales force under a director of service marketing or sales. In general, the direct sales organization, as well as the indirect sales force, will make use of the merchandising and packaging mechanisms described above to support the selling process and close sales. It is important to recognize that defining the service portfolio and targeting market segments directly contribute to the achievement of maximum efficiency in presenting the services to users. These steps also accelerate and improve the process of closing a sale and making a contract commitment.

The Development Process for a Service Marketing Strategy

In summary, the development and implementation of a successful marketing strategy for service operations involves four sequential but related steps:

1. Establishing the service portfolio
2. Establishing service portfolio prices through market segmentation and focus
3. Merchandising and packaging the service portfolio
4. Selling the service portfolio by means of the merchandising and packaging mechanisms

The development and implementation of a marketing strategy is a continuous process. Feedback from customers by market segment is used to adjust the marketing focus and service portfolio definitions, prices, and merchandising and selling mechanisms to meet present and emerging needs and competition. A formal and precise marketing and pricing strategy should be utilized that is based upon a full commitment to market research, analysis, and evaluation. The optimal service is critically dependent upon market perceptions; it is important for a service organization to understand and measure these perceptions by market segment and use this understanding as a basis for developing and implementing a successful marketing strategy.

7
Pricing Service

One of the most important decisions facing the managers of service organizations is the determination of prices. In industries dealing with the manufacture, distribution, and delivery of *tangible goods*, the long-term economic strategy is to base the prices on the costs of manufacturing and/or distributing the goods plus the ordinary markup for overhead and profit. This is primarily dictated by the concept of a production learning curve* for goods and by the consumer's preference for purchasing the lowest-priced equivalent goods. In essence, cost-plus pricing is the general strategic pricing policy for tangible goods, with some possible variations employed "tactically" (e.g., setting prices that are lower than the prices of major competitors with the lowest, or "best," learning curve) to gain market share for competitive advantage in the short run. In general, in many markets, this approach to pricing has also been utilized by the service industry, particularly in the establishment of prices for equipment maintenance and repair services.

Avoiding the Tendency to Underprice Services

However, the cost-plus pricing strategy often leads companies to *underprice* their service products and capabilities. The primary reasons include:

*A *production learning curve* describes the change in unit cost of production as the producing agency manufactures greater numbers of units, thereby achieving economies of scale and improved efficiency and productivity per unit. Typically, a learning curve shows a nonlinear decrease in unit costs as production volume increases.

130

1. *Failure to recognize price-insensitive or price-inelastic market segments.* Considerable research has demonstrated that with respect to service quality and response, a significant percentage of customers (close to 40 percent) are relatively *price-insensitive or price-inelastic.* A significant percentage of the market is therefore much more concerned about the *quality of service* than about price. In fact, some segments actually view price as a surrogate for quality and presume that lower-priced service means lower quality of delivery.

2. *Laziness of marketing and sales personnel.* It is obviously much easier to sell lower-priced services (as well as products), and most sales personnel concerned about product sales tend to "give away" services in order to gain product sales.

3. *Fear of market reaction.* There is a continuing fear on the part of service personnel that higher prices will not "stick" or that the market will react negatively. This "gut" reaction is often dictated by experiences in product markets as opposed to service, but the fear remains.

There are a number of other problems associated with the utilization of pricing strategies adapted from product-oriented industries. These include:

1. *Creation of competitive disadvantages.* The general cost-plus-markup approach used in most pricing decisions tends to generate competitive disadvantages if service managers fail to recognize that there are different economies of scale or cost advantages with different sizes or structures of service organizations. Typically, the large service organizations, which are market leaders, have made significant investments in systems for centralized call handling, remote diagnostics technology, and integrated logistics; they have therefore lowered their cost of operations. Smaller service organizations, or those organizations which have not made similar technological investments, often fail to recognize the differences in economies of scale or cost advantages; therefore, the use of the cost-plus-markup approach tends to result in prices which are significantly higher than the prices of the major competitors, with no difference in the quality of service delivered.

2. *Incorrect cost information.* A major problem in service pricing is the lack of knowledge of the true costs of service products or of service by market segment. Very few firms have developed cost allocation mechanisms which can identify the *true costs* associated with short, midrange, and long response times, or service by market segment, or the type of service.

3. *Inattention to pricing issues, both strategic and tactical.* Many or-

ganizations do not track either the tactical or strategic (long-term) trends in pricing. They fail to recognize underlying changes in market structure and/or price competition.

4. *Inconsistencies in pricing in order to maintain a full service line.*   Many firms recognize the importance of providing an integrated portfolio of services. This, however, may require the sale of some services at a loss until significant volume can be built up to achieve economies of scale. Pricing each of the individual service lines within the portfolio on a cost-plus-markup basis can therefore lead to significant inconsistencies in the overall pricing strategy.

5. *Inappropriate goals.*   Finally, many service managers fail to recognize that pricing is an important vehicle for achieving goals—e.g., maximizing current profits, maximizing long-term profits, gaining market share, or erecting barriers to the entry of competitors. In the equipment service market, where the long-term cost of service (over the life cycle) may be considerably higher than the purchase price of the product for which the service is provided, these goals are particularly important. It is essential that the pricing strategy be based upon an understanding and definition of the strategic goals. Dropping service prices *merely* to sell products in the short run is, for example, an inappropriate goal if the analysis fails to consider the total loss and/or gain over the product life cycle. In general, the cost-plus pricing approach fails to differentiate between such short- and long-term impacts and alternatives.

In summary, service organizations need to consider a number of issues that affect service pricing. Then they can consider alternative pricing mechanisms.

Pricing Strategy Alternatives

In broad terms, there are three mechanisms available for establishing service prices:

- *Cost plus markup.*   This approach is primarily driven by the cost of operation. It involves determining the direct cost of the service and adding a normal markup for overhead and profit.
- *Competitive pricing.*   This approach is primarily driven by competitive prices, with typical emphasis on the market leader. Usually, prices are set as some percentage of (either less than or equal to) the market leader's prices.
- *Value-in-use pricing.*   This third approach generally involves focus-

ing on the value to the customer of the service to be provided, measured particularly in the absence of the service.

A summary of the service pricing alternatives and the advantages and disadvantages of each is presented in Table 7-1. The procedures for establishing service prices under these alternatives are described below.

Cost-Plus Pricing Strategy

The cost-plus pricing strategy could be developed on the basis of the analysis of actual results, if the cost accounting system does provide the level of detail required. A cost-plus modeling approach can generally be utilized in the absence of a full cost accounting system. A typical fully loaded service cost model is driven by the hourly labor rate, the incidence of occurrence of service calls, service time, and the desired gross profit level (see Fig. 7-1). The general model also uses the reliability or failure characteristics of the equipment (mean time between failures—MTBF) and the targeted service response time (mean time to repair—MTTR). There is generally a reasonably high correlation between service response time and the utilization level of the service force. While these relationships will obviously vary as a function of equipment density, geographic area, and other factors, the quantitative parameters shown in Fig. 7-2 represent a reasonable average in the United States.

Figure 7-3 presents an example of the calculations involved in computing annual maintenance price on a cost-plus basis, utilizing this model. For a product with an MTBF of 325 hours* and an MTTR of about 3 hours, the calculations lead to an annual service charge of $3775.

More elaborate cost-plus models can be developed and utilized. However, the cost-plus model presented here provides a good rule of thumb for calculating service price for most high-tech products. It is important to note that the cost-plus model tends to be somewhat sensitive to the mean time between failures or the mean time between service calls. As the equipment becomes more reliable, the cost-plus model tends to dictate that service prices should drop.

Competitive Pricing

Many service organizations tend to use a pricing approach which is based on an assessment of major competitors' prices. For example, the

---

*This could also be used for the mean time between service (MTBS).

Table 7-1. Service Pricing Alternatives

Pricing strategy	Approach	Advantages	Disadvantages
Cost-plus	Determine MTBF, MTTR, travel time, and labor rate to arrive at price.	Ensures coverage of costs.	Fails to provide service quality based on customer needs. Fails to provide basis for pricing to different segments.
Competitive	Determine price of major competitor, and price the same or under.	Provides some competitive advantage in the short run.	May cause perception bias; cheaper service means lower quality. Actual revenue may produce lower quality when the organization is competing with an efficient firm.
Value-in-use	Determine cost to customer in absence of service; provide service based on targeted market segment needs.	Directly satisfies customer needs and requirements for service at reasonable price based on customer values.	Requires market research to measure values. May not be competitive in price-sensitive market.

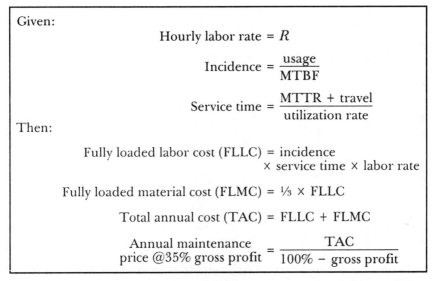

Figure 7-1. Fully loaded service cost model. (MTBF = mean time between failures; MTTR = mean time to repair.)

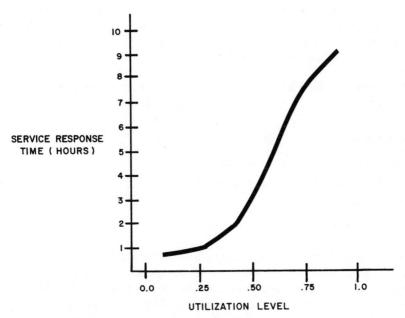

Figure 7-2. Service response time versus utilization rate.

Incidence:

$$\text{MTBF} = 325 \text{ hours}$$

$$\text{Usage} = 2000 \text{ hours}$$

Service time:

$$\text{MTTR} = 2.75 \text{ hours}$$

$$\text{Travel} = 1.00 \text{ hour}$$

$$\text{Utilization rate} = 50\%$$

$$\text{Fully loaded labor rate} = \$40$$

$$\text{Gross profit objective} = 35\%$$

$$\text{FLLC} = \frac{2000}{325} \times \frac{3.75}{0.50} \times \$40 = \$1845$$

$$\text{FLMC} = 0.33 \times \$1846 = \$609$$

$$\text{TAC} = \$1846 + \$609 = \$2454$$

$$\text{Annual maintenance price} = \frac{\$2455}{1.00 - 0.35} = \$3775$$

Figure 7-3. Sample service price calculations based on the cost-plus model.

rule of thumb in most high-tech product markets is to use a figure that is 7 to 11 percent of the purchase price as the annual maintenance charge. This is viewed as the "competitive" price. The basic factors influencing competitive pricing include:

1. The basic service charge of the major competitor, which is usually equal to or less than the smaller and less efficient competitor's basic cost
2. Surcharges for extended coverage
3. Surcharges for improved response
4. Surcharges for expanded geography
5. Other special charges
6. Surcharges for uptime guarantee

There are a number of difficulties in using the competitive pricing approach to strategically establish service prices. My in-depth analysis of competitive pricing for equipment service clearly shows both a lack of consistency in service pricing and significant differences in the final service price as a function of the "ups and adds."* For example, in the computer services field, an examination of the major competitor's basic annual maintenance charge (BAMC) as a percentage of purchase price shows significant differences, particularly as equipment prices drop. The percentage is simply not linear.

The nonlinear character of this curve is clearly not well understood by many managers in service businesses. They tend to view competitive prices *on the average* without understanding the underlying driving elements. For example, in the computer market, an averaging of IBM's service prices as a percentage of purchase price would tend to give the rule-of-thumb figure of 7 to 11 percent, which is often used as an industry standard. However, this is not at all the rationale used by the major competitor. In fact, a more general analysis of competitive maintenance prices, including consideration of "ups and adds," shows that the BAMC, while an important factor in determining competitive price, is only a part of the overall equation. Typically, the major competitor in any service market uses a complex pricing approach based on its particular market interests; it charges less in some areas where it wants greater market penetration or control, and it charges more in other segments when it already has control. Competitive pricing requires an in-depth assessment of the major competitor's pricing strategy rather than reliance on simple rules of thumb.

Value-in-Use Pricing

The third pricing approach—the one that is most applicable to equipment service—is value-in-use pricing. The value-in-use approach is customer-centered rather than competitor- or cost-centered. Until recently, service pricing has been protected by the product price and the service performance "umbrella" [i.e., the offer of the "industry standard" for service, or the service offer of the primary competitor(s)]. However, with the cost of service and support representing an increasing percentage of the total life-cycle cost of ownership (well above 50 percent today), this approach is rapidly changing. In essence, the customer is increasingly examining the full cost of ownership with a heavier focus on service prices as a function of service quality.

Recognizing the differences in required service response and repair times for different market segments is the key to the value-in-use pricing approach. For example, one can calculate the full cost of downtime by considering the number of types of users, the hours per day and

---

*That is, other surcharges that are imposed as features or performance levels beyond the basic service portfolio are added.

days per week of operations, the incidence of downtime, the average length of downtime, and the impact of downtime. The service price is then determined by computing the value of a given service portfolio to the individual market segment as a result of offsetting the cost of downtime. This value will be significantly higher for the larger user with a critical dependence on service versus the smaller user or those for whom uptime is not critical. These calculations must then be tested against competitive prices and modified if the service portfolio is exactly the same as one currently provided at a lower competitive price. The ultimate value-in-use pricing approach is thus determined by the value to the individual user segment of minimizing downtime at a reasonable cost, as a function of service quality (i.e., time) parameters.

The *major difference* between cost-plus and competitive pricing, on the one hand, and value-in-use pricing, on the other, is that value-in-use pricing is based on an explicit definition of *service portfolio quality and delivery capability*, whereas cost-plus and competitive pricing are generally based on an *average level of service response.*

Relating User Types to Pricing Strategies

In establishing an optimum price for the individual components of the service portfolio, it is important to recognize that in the typical market, at least three classes of users can be identified:

1. *Standard-service customers.*   These users require *basic*, or standard, services and are concerned primarily about the cost of service.

2. *Quality-service customers.*   These users want to ensure that service delivery and performance will be of a *reasonable* quality and that service costs will also be reasonable.

3. *Premium-service customers.*   These users require service that is significantly better than standard or quality service and are willing to pay a *premium*, or higher amount, to *guarantee* quality performance in the future.

The general characterization of these three classes of customers (Table 7-2) can be determined in individual markets through market research, analysis, and evaluation. For example, answers to a specific survey question used in the information technology market suggest that approximately 10 percent of users fall into the *standard* segment; approximately 50 percent are in the *quality* segment; and the remaining 40 percent (a *significant* minority) are in the *premium* segment. (See

Table 7-2. Classes of Service Users

Service user type	Service requirements	Service price elasticity
Premium	Very high Response time and repair time: 1 to 3 hours	Very low Willing to pay significant premium to obtain quality service
Quality	High Response time and repair time: 3 to 5 hours	Average Willing to pay reasonable increase to obtain quality service
Standard	Low to medium Response time and repair time: 8 hours or more	High Not willing to pay premium; prefer to pay less and would be willing to accept some reduction in service

Fig. 7-4 for an example of a market survey question used in the information technology market.)

The importance of service pricing is easier to understand when one examines the price and performance elasticity distributions for these standard, quality, and premium classes of customers by market segment. The establishment of specific *alternative* service portfolios and appropriate pricing for each of the three classes of customers by market segment can provide an optimum revenue and profit margin contribution for service and, at the same time, optimize the levels of customer satisfaction. Extensive market research clearly indicates that the extent of service price elasticity will be related to factors associated with (1) product, (2) market segment or structure, and (3) product use. The primary *strategic implications* of service price elasticity by type of customer relate to the opportunity to achieve higher revenues and profit margins in specific market segments and for specific product lines. In general, the price of service should be based on whichever is *higher*—value in use or cost plus markup. Since, in most markets, service price is not as important as service performance, cost-plus or competitive service pricing is generally *not* the optimum (i.e., most profitable) service pricing strategy. Those market segments which have a high value in use for service and for which service demand is highly inelastic present the most profitable market opportunities.

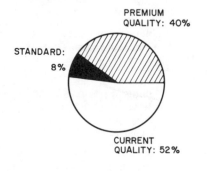

QUESTION:

IT IS EXPECTED THAT SERVICE PRICES IN THE INFORMATION TECHNOLOGY MARKET WILL INCREASE AS A RESULT OF DEREGULATION, INCREASING LABOR COSTS, ETC. WHEN PRICES CHANGE, YOU MIGHT PREFER TO PURCHASE DIFFERENT SERVICE OPTIONS. PLEASE SELECT THE OPTION WHICH YOU WOULD MOST LIKELY PURCHASE.

OPTION:	RESPONSE
• IMPROVED, PREMIUM SERVICE AT A PREMIUM OR SIGNIFICANTLY HIGHER PRICE	40%
• CURRENT-QUALITY SERVICE AT AN INCREASED PRICE	52%
• LOWER-STANDARD SERVICE AT CURRENT PRICE	8%
TOTAL	100%

CONCLUSION: LESS THAN 10% OF ALL SURVEY RESPONDENTS ARE WILLING TO SACRIFICE SERVICE PERFORMANCE IN ORDER TO REDUCE THE COST; IN FACT, A SIGNIFICANT PERCENTAGE ARE WILLING TO PAY A PREMIUM (HIGHER) PRICE FOR PREMIUM-QUALITY SERVICE.

Figure 7-4. Price sensitivity of service users in the information technology market.

Effects of Alternative Pricing Strategies

A detailed evaluation of alternative pricing strategies in a wide variety of markets clearly shows the general framework of pricing strategies and their impact on users and vendors. As shown in Fig. 7-5, the typical annual maintenance charges as a function of a major parameter associated with use, such as the number of users, will ultimately be driven, at the lower end of the scale, by the cost-plus approach. However, as the number of users (or service criticality) increases, significant changes occur with respect to the optimum price under a cost-plus, competitive, or value-in-use approach. The value-in-use price will generally be at the highest level. This does not mean that the higher value-in-use price is at a *competitive economic disadvantage* relative to the other two prices. Value-in-use prices can be higher because of the key element of service quality embedded in the value-in-use pricing strategy. In essence, because of the increasing importance of the service portfolio *quality*, a significant percentage of users (i.e., those who are price-insensitive or price-inelastic) will opt for the value-in-use price, even though it is significantly higher than either the competitive price or the cost-plus price.

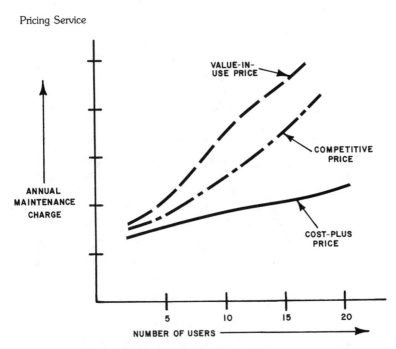

Figure 7-5. Comparison of alternative pricing strategies.

Increasing a Price Is Easier than Lowering It

Service pricing must become much more sophisticated if service organizations are to survive and prevail in the growing service market. It is important to recognize the existence of alternative approaches to pricing, with particular emphasis on the value-in-use approach. In the traditional cost-plus approach or in competitive pricing, there is a great tendency toward price reductions. However, as indicated in Fig. 7-6, *it is extremely important to note* that one must achieve a *significant increase* in sales volume as a result of even a minor price reduction in order to maintain the same gross profit margin that existed before the price change. This analysis suggests that price reductions require a significant increase in selling effort in order to maintain the same gross profit margin. For example, at a 35 percent gross profit margin, a price reduction of 10 percent requires more than a 40 percent increase in unit sales. On the other hand, an increase in price can support a *significant decrease* in sales volume without hurting the gross profit margin. For example, at a 35 percent gross profit margin, a price increase of 10 percent can result in a *decrease* of 20 percent or more in sales volume without affecting the previous gross profit margin.

Service managers should be extremely careful in developing service

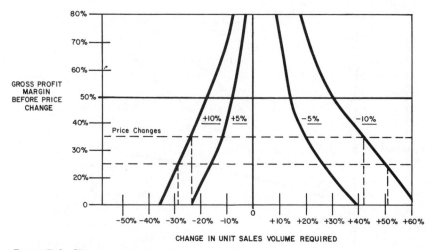

Figure 7-6. Change in unit sales volume required to offset a change in gross profit that results from a change in unit price.

prices and particularly in *reducing* service prices in the face of competition in order to gain market share. My in-depth market research clearly shows that a significant percentage of the market is price-insensitive. Thus, in general, the development of service prices should be driven by the calculation of value in use as well as by competitive and cost-plus pricing strategies. These three pricing alternatives should then be compared in order to determine:

1. The desirability of a *price increase* for the higher quality required by the targeted market segment, in order to *increase revenue and profits*

2. The desirability of *maintaining a competitive price* for the higher quality (dictated by the value in use) required by the market, in order to gain market share

Service pricing strategies are extremely complex. Value-in-use pricing can result in significantly higher profit margins with essentially the same service quality. It can also be used to achieve a significant increase in market penetration and market share through a focus on the defined service quality parameters required by the *key* vertical market segments.

8

Managing and Controlling Service

Service as a Strategic Business: Key Organizational and Operational Concepts

Service needs to be managed and controlled efficiently. The real key to establishing a strategically driven service organization seems almost too simple: define the service functions to be performed by the strategic service unit, and make sure someone has total responsibility for management and control. It is very difficult to describe service in operational terms. We all seem to have a general understanding of what service is. However, describing the most *effective* and efficient organizational and operational structure to control and deliver service is difficult. Quite often, service activities are decentralized, with no one executive or manager truly responsible for management, control, coordination, or resource allocation. These are the steps to follow to set up and effectively manage service:

1. Identify the service functions.

2. Establish the operational framework for delivery of the functions.

3. Place a service-oriented, experienced manager in charge.

Service generally involves three major functions:

- *Service task or problem identification, scheduling, and assignment.* Service generally starts with the identification and description of a task or problem, the identification of the resources needed to sat-

143

isfy the requirement, and the assignment of the resources to resolve the requirement.

- *Service task performance.* The field resources needed to complete the service task, generally including people and materials or parts, must be deployed and managed. In day-to-day terms, this function also includes tracking the resource status to ensure compliance with the service requirement and closing out the service call upon completion of the task.
- *Service support.* Service performance generally also requires some type of infrastructure support, including, but not limited to:
  1. Technical assistance
  2. Documentation
  3. Training
  4. Logistics and parts-related support, including depot repair and refurbishment
  5. Marketing and communications
  6. Service contract administration
  7. Financial and accounting coordination and control
  8. Data management and reporting
  9. Other specific services, such as systems integration, design and engineering, consultation, and catastrophic backup

A service organization must have a management structure to support these three key functions. Equally important is the need to have systems and procedures which can provide control of the service operations in accordance with the time targets of the service portfolio. Systems and procedures are also needed to organize, store, and retrieve the data which are critical for day-to-day and long-term decision making.

Thus, for example, the service organization of a manufacturing firm should include:

- *The customer service or call-handling operation* (for identifying the task or problem and scheduling resources)
- *The service force in the field* (for performing the service task)
- *The logistics and technical support groups* (for providing service support)

Similar structures exist for other types of service organizations, such as airlines, hospitals, and restaurants (see Table 8-1). In each case, the critical problem is to identify the three key service functions and then define and implement the organizational elements that are necessary for managing these functions to provide service for the customers.

Table 8-1. Examples of Elements of Service Organizations

	Types of service organizations				
Major functions	Manufacturer service	Airline	Hospital	Restaurant
Service task or problem identification, scheduling, and assignment	Customer service or call-handling desk	Reservations center	Admissions office	Maître d' or host
Service task performance	Field service engineers	Pilots	Doctors and nurses	Waiters and waitresses
Service support	Logistics and technical support groups	Maintenance force Support personnel Flight attendants Passenger representatives Baggage handlers	Diagnostic imaging services Other support services	Cooks

Key Organizational Elements

To facilitate the strategic management of service, a service organization should place the key service functions under a single designated manager and have a formal system for supporting the functions and providing data on service performance, customer needs and requirements, and service costs. For a simple service operation, the functions can be organized on a straightforward basis. For example, in a restaurant, the maître d' is normally responsible for service call handling and scheduling, the waiters and waitresses perform the service tasks, and the kitchen staff (cooks, helpers, dishwashers, etc.) provide the service support.

In some cases, the functions of service task identification and service task performance may be combined. In a bank, hotel, or airline reservations service, for example, the teller, desk clerk, or reservations clerk makes the initial decision about the need for service and then goes on to provide the service required. However, as the service responsibilities grow and become more formalized, it becomes critical to separate out the initial service identification function and to improve the systems support associated with the function. This is especially true in equipment service, where the effectiveness of problem identification can have a significant impact on service response time and the efficiency of service delivery and performance.

To provide full service capability, a service business must create an organizational structure similar to the general structure shown in Fig. 8-1. It should include the basic functions associated with overall service management and the three key service functions: service identification (call handling), direct service performance (usually organized geographically, at the regional or local level, for larger service organizations), and service support. While there can easily be variations in this organizational structure, the key elements which must be present are as follows:

- One senior executive who can make the key decisions regarding service levels, service performance, and service budget allocations

- Clear lines of authority and responsibility for each major part of the service equation (i.e., identification and assignment, performance, and support)

- Defined procedures for satisfying specific customer needs and requirements for service

- All resources required to provide service, with a single manager responsible for those resources

- A well-defined contact point between the customer and the service organization

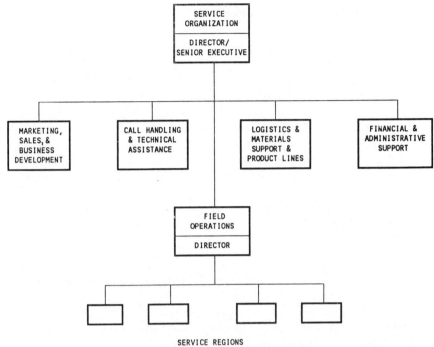

Figure 8-1. A typical service organization structure.

For most service businesses, the most important element of the organizational structure is the contact point: a customer needs clear access to the service organization to report service needs and obtain service assistance. The organization must be oriented, from top to bottom, to customer requirements and needs, with a full commitment to quality service performance. The personnel of the service organization must be motivated to fully meet customer service requests on both a disciplined and cost-effective basis.

This *total commitment* to service can be obtained through:

- *Education and training* of the service staff and management in customer needs and requirements
- *Incentive compensation* based on perceived and actual service performance, evaluated according to customer-driven measures
- *Use of management systems and procedures* for full coordination and control, with particular emphasis on the management of service time and the establishment of specific time targets for individual service tasks

Service Management Requirements and Functions

A service organization must be managed by an individual with experience in service and a commitment to customers. Perhaps most important, the service executive or manager must be able to understand both the *external* customer requirements and needs and the *internal* service operation and delivery capability and then manage the critical balance between the two. This requires the ability to work with the internal service staff and a strong willingness and capability to deal with external customers and customer issues. Experience and training in service marketing, business development, and service management systems are also very desirable.

The key management issues and control questions outlined below define the scope of the service manager's role. Service operations must be managed and coordinated on two levels:

1. *Strategic level.* The strategy for service operations involves decisions about levels of service and responsiveness to be provided and the resolution of a wide range of questions about staffing levels and skills, territory assignments, inventory levels, and inventory allocations to national and/or regional depots and customer service field support kits. These issues must be analyzed and managed through the use of a model of the service environment reflecting both internal capabilities and external (customer) needs. The model can be informal, at a conceptual level within the service manager's overall viewpoint, or formalized as a framework for analysis. Operational tracking and reporting systems can provide the key data on service performance and needs. Under either analytical framework, a management system should be used to coordinate the strategy for service and to manage and control that strategy. The management system provides the time and procedural discipline which is critical to the successful execution of the service model as conceived.

2. *Tactical and operational level.* Within the context of the strategy for service operations, the service organization is faced with the day-to-day, hour-by-hour decisions and problems associated with the coordination, control, and allocation of service calls. The typical service executive must provide the decision framework and policy for on-line control and coordination of service staff, as well as similar capabilities with respect to the control of service support, including inventory (parts) and other technical resources at the point of use.

The Call-Handling, Assignment, and Dispatch Function

At least two major functions must be strategically and tactically controlled in the service organization. These include the call-handling, assignment, and dispatch function and the logistics and parts and materials support function (which will be discussed in the next major section of this chapter).

In the typical service organization, the process of problem identification and assignment starts the action in which a customer service person is assigned to a set of accounts and products and a geographic area, or territory. Customers requiring service will contact their assigned service specialists or a service center. For those service centers serving large populations (e.g., an area office), the call-handling and dispatch function is usually performed on a centralized, regional, or local basis. The call-handling function can be carried out by a single individual or by a large staff, using advanced systems and technology.

As a service organization grows, so does the need for more sophisticated and disciplined call handling, dispatching, data collection, and resource management and control. For most control purposes, self-dispatching* is not desirable, particularly if there is an issue of service problem identification and definition (i.e., if the service requirement is not well defined or can be handled in more than one way or by more than one set of resources). Experience has shown that specialized technology (such as artificial intelligence and advanced diagnostics) can be especially useful for service problem identification and resolution. I will discuss this technology in more detail in Chap. 9.

The requirements for adequate management reporting will also become crucial as a service organization grows. A larger service organization will normally need some type of hierarchical structure for administrative control (e.g., all service personnel report to area offices, and all area offices are under a regional office). These considerations require the development of a formalized, disciplined approach to service reporting on the status of call handling, dispatch, and call resolution. Such an approach should be developed in the context of a strategic operating plan related to required levels of service and responsiveness. In this way, reports on performance can be directly compared with service objectives, by organizational level, to highlight where service was performed within planned targets and where it was not. Service operations

---

*That is, letting the service person decide, without specific guidance, how and in what time frame to provide service.

managers must decide on the strategy to be employed for managing call handling and dispatch. This strategy should be based on four broad issues:

1. *Level of call taking and dispatch coordination.* All service calls must be taken, processed, and assigned. For a small or simple service operation, such as a single restaurant, this is an easy issue, since calls are obviously handled at that one location. However, for large or complex service operations, particularly when service is provided in more than one location, the question of the best level for call handling and dispatch needs to be examined in the context of the cost of operations, the ability to provide full-time call-handling coverage, the economies of scale to be derived through centralization, and the degree of flexibility and responsiveness which can be obtained through centralized, regional, or local communication. In general, if individual customer needs do not vary significantly, or if they can be communicated and defined through some type of call management system, the *centralized* approach is best. However, if customer requirements vary widely and service performance must be specifically tailored, the local or regional approach works best.

2. *Call avoidance and remote diagnostics.* The full call-handling function involves problem identification and the determination of the optimum service response, which could include providing direct advice for the customer, thereby eliminating the need for the service call altogether (call avoidance). The critical questions are as follows:

- What possibilities for call avoidance exist? Do all requests for assistance require full service action, or can some problems be resolved by the call taker?
- What mechanisms and technology (such as artificial intelligence) exist which can be used to identify problems and avoid service calls?
- What procedures for employing call-avoidance mechanisms exist?

We need to examine the flow of calls requesting service to determine how to handle them efficiently, in the least time and with the smallest expense. If the above questions are asked and the answers indicate that some service calls can be avoided and that specific avoidance mechanisms exist and can be employed, we have taken the first step toward making total call handling more efficient and effective.

3. *Call dispatch procedures.* Once a decision has been made to provide full or partial assignment to a service call, the next step is to formally establish the procedures to make the service call assignment efficiently. Typical dispatch procedures include:

- *First come, first served.*   Deal with the first person requesting service first.
- *Preassigned site and/or customer.*   Make an assignment or schedule for a customer and/or service location in advance; in effect, have a reservation system.
- *Highest-priority customer.*   Establish priorities, in terms of special classes or segments of customers or service users; always process a higher-priority customer before a lower-priority customer.
- *Target response times.*   Examine all service requests occurring at a given time, and dispatch calls so that all requests are handled within a given time response target.
- *Customer satisfaction.*   Establish different service levels for different customers on the basis of their needs and requirements, or their willingness to pay, or some combination of the two; dispatch to first satisfy the most critical or time-sensitive needs of customers willing to pay the most.

The simplest procedure—first come, first served—is the one that is most often applied. However, it is often *not* the best choice, particularly where different customers using the same service organization have different service needs, service time requests or priorities, and/or willingness to pay. We need to recognize the existence of the other dispatch procedures and explore how and under what conditions each procedure might be used. It should be noted that some combination of dispatch procedures could be employed. For example, we could first segment customers on the basis of need and then process requests on a first-come, first-served basis.

4. *Assignment of service personnel.*   The fourth call-handling issue is the actual assignment process. Service operations managers must decide how to assign service tasks to the service force in order to best meet customer requirements and needs, maintain efficiency, and optimize cost effectiveness. There are four major assignment methods:

- *Territory or customer assignment.*   Assign a specific service person to a specific area or customer. This approach tends to emphasize knowledge of the customer and the customer's environment.
- *Product or technology assignment.*   Assign a service person on the basis of product or technology knowledge. This approach tends to emphasize technical skill.
- *Dynamic assignment.*   Assign a service person on the basis of the goal of minimizing elapsed service time (waiting time) for each customer, taking into account technical knowledge and skills required and available, as well as knowledge of the customer. This approach emphasizes the need to dynamically balance skills and knowledge against elapsed service time.

- *Service escalation.*   The service personnel should be able to report on the status of their assigned service calls. If the service is not completed within the given service objective (usually expressed as a time target in minutes or hours), an "alert" mechanism should be used to send a report on the problem to the next higher service management level. These key operational reports (e.g., reports on mean time between failures, service response time distribution, and service engineer utilization) should be available to provide management with an overview of call-handling and dispatch performance against customer service targets, including exceptional performance that exceeds service goals.

The Seven Steps Involved in the Call-Handling and Dispatch Function

Figure 8-2 shows the general flow of the activities designed to support the call-handling and dispatch function. This function involves seven basic steps:

1. *Entry of service.*   The call taker records the request for service, including the identification of the customer.

2. *Analysis and evaluation of problem.*   Formal procedures and historical data are used to determine whether the service issue can be re-

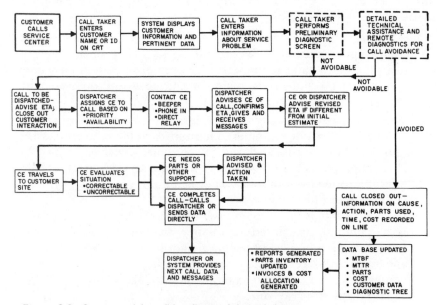

Figure 8-2. Overview of the call-handling and dispatch function.

solved immediately or whether full-service action is necessary. If the call taker provides the customer with an immediate service solution, the call can be closed out; otherwise, the customer needs an estimated service action time and a commitment to resolve the problem. This step is extremely critical, for at this stage the use of procedures and data can be most helpful in resolving the problem to the customer's satisfaction without the full deployment of more expensive resources. In the absence of such action, the service request can easily become a message that is passed from one office of the service organization to another, resulting in increasing customer dissatisfaction and rising costs. Under any circumstances, the call taker should either resolve the issue directly or provide the customer with clear information as to when and how the service will be provided.

3. *Dispatch and assignment.* If the evaluation results in the decision to assign a service person, the next step is the actual assignment of the service person, on the basis of specific allocation rules, procedures, and priorities. The dispatch and assignment should take into account the customer's service requirement, the service person's ability (and the resources available) to meet that requirement, and the service calls still unassigned.

4. *Monitoring and closing out of service calls.* The fourth step is the continuous, dynamic monitoring of all service requests and service force assignments and, ultimately, the closing out of completed service actions. Here again, a procedure other than simply first come, first served can have a high payoff. Improvements in dispatch and assignment can be gained by examining the willingness of individual customers to wait shorter or longer periods of time; by establishing different priorities of customers on the basis of willingness to pay, value in use of service, or some other criterion; and by considering the probable time for service completion.

5. *Action alert and management intervention.* All service requirements should be continually monitored through a call-activity reporting and tracking system. A controlled escalation of service resources should be provided in the event that the service response objectives are not being met. This management intervention and escalation with respect to the dispatch and assignment of service personnel is a critical feedback mechanism. It is important to formally establish this mechanism to ensure a full commitment of the service organization to the customer base.

6. *Service data maintenance.* This step involves the continuous updating and maintenance of the data associated with the call-handling and tracking process, service staff status, customer status, and product status. The processing and evaluation of service data can help a service organization anticipate service problems, initiate actions to prevent the

occurrence of uncontrolled service tasks, and forecast service demands. Accurate processing of service calls to link service requirements or needs with corrective action can provide insight and aids for improving the effectiveness of the initial analysis and evaluation of problems (step 2). I will discuss this use of data for call diagnostics later in this chapter.

7. *Generation of service reports.* A service organization needs hourly, daily, weekly, and monthly reports on service performance and activities so that it can determine whether it is meeting targets, goals, and objectives.

In general, as shown in Fig. 8-2, a disciplined process should be used to handle a call, from the customer's request for service through analysis and evaluation of the problem, service dispatch and assignment, and the completion and reporting of the call, regardless of the service environment or situation. This call-handling process could be very informal in a restaurant or retail shop, more elaborate and disciplined in a bank or insurance firm, and very precise and elaborate in a high-technology service and support organization. It is most important to handle the evaluation and assignment steps as key service decisions in the context of a knowledge of the customer's service requirements and to use the capability to examine service history in order to forecast real requirements.

Implementing the Call-Handling and Dispatch Function

There are several specific management alternatives which should be considered in fully implementing an optimum call-handling and dispatch function. The possible choices are covered in the following pages.

Centralization versus Decentralization. As I pointed out earlier, the location of the call-handling and dispatch function [i.e., at the national (or central), regional, or local level] will affect both service efficiencies and cost. Many service organizations do not have a uniform policy with respect to call handling and dispatch. The typical practice is informal, ad hoc call handling and dispatch at the local level. In many cases, calls are made directly to, and handled directly by, an individual service person. However, this may often lead to a less efficient service process, as the service person attempts to resolve the customer's problem without taking into account priorities, other resources available, etc. A local answering service is sometimes employed. While the cost of this type of call handling is generally low, the key ability to diagnose and perhaps resolve the problem at the time of the customer's call is generally lacking. For a large service organization or one providing broad service coverage, the most efficient approach is *national*, or *central*, call handling and dispatch. All other options typically require more computing equipment, higher telecommunications costs, and/or additional staff to achieve a given level of call-handling and dispatch capability.*

However, centralization can often lead to less direct supervisory involvement and a reduction in service flexibility. Local service supervisors generally know the specific requirements and needs of individual customers. Specific steps should therefore be taken to ensure that the centralized call-handling function allows local service supervisors to explicitly identify and describe special exceptions and priorities. One way to achieve this is by improving field communications. Also, the use of computers and a data network system can allow the introduction of specific parameters, constraints, and guidelines, to be established by *local* and/or regional service managers; this will improve supervisory control of the priorities and special customer-handling procedures in the actual dispatch process at the central level. Improvements in supervisory control can be achieved at any level, including the local or regional level. Direct access to call status and specific customer situations can be provided for regional or local service managers through a computer display screen or printer, thus maintaining local supervisory control. The call-handling and dispatch function should be designed on a modular basis so that control can be decentralized if local call handling and/or dispatch is deemed desirable by management, or if the greater flexibility provided by local assignment is required and cannot be provided by alternative means.

A full assessment of the trade-offs involving national, regional, and local call handling and dispatch, shown in Table 8-2, suggests that the most cost-effective solution is national-level call handling and dispatch.

Levels of Operational Performance. In general, given the seven steps of the call-handling and dispatch function defined above, one of three operational approaches for implementation can be chosen, depending on the size and sophistication of the service organization and the needs and requirements of the customers.

Minimum, or Basic, Approach. A basic approach to general call handling involves a very simple call opening; usually manual dispatch and assignment on a first-come, first-served basis; and a simple report or completion of the invoice in closing out the service task. This approach is used in simple service businesses—e.g., a restaurant, a laundry, or a very small (5- to 10-person) field service operation.

Intermediate-Level Approach. The second, or intermediate-level, approach typically involves all seven steps in the call-handling and dispatch function. More explicit data on each service call are usually ob-

---

*In general, all other options would cost a minimum of 10 to 20 percent more for equipment and communications, plus at least 20 percent more in staffing support costs.

Table 8-2. Evaluation of Centralization versus Decentralization Options for Call Handling and Dispatch

Call handling and dispatch	Requests for service		
	National (central) level	Regional level	Local (district or branch) level
National (central) level	Least costly alternative with potential for managed control of service	Viable, but requires greater communications costs	Viable, but low productivity option for staff
Regional level	Viable, but requires greater communications costs	Viable, but requires greater investment in staff	Viable, but high communications and data processing costs
Local (district or branch) level	Viable, but low productivity option for staff	Viable, but high communications and data processing costs	Viable, but requires greatest investment in facilities Offers greatest potential for improving staff productivity

tained and used for billing, cost accounting, and call diagnostics. Parts usage data are usually collected and reported. At this level, the processing of the call is more formal and generally involves a dedicated call-handling person or staff. Some level of automation may be provided, allowing simple staff-machine interaction and formal procedures for recording and tracking the open calls and completed calls, with specific reporting on time, costs, parts and materials, and service activities. The intermediate-level approach for implementing call handling and dispatch is normally used in small service organizations and in the decentralized operations of larger service organizations.

Advanced-Level Approach. At the advanced level, the call-handling and dispatch function usually possesses some "intelligence" about service history and about previous relationships between problems, symptoms, causes, and corrective actions. This function also has a full management role, primarily for making formal decisions about the need for full-service dispatch and assignment and the development of specific recommendations for action. This may include determination down to a specific individual, taking into account skill levels, parts, etc. At the advanced level, there is generally full processing support (i.e., more automation) of all the call-handling steps. In addition, there is direct, in-depth diagnostics based on data developed from previous calls relating problems and symptoms to causes and corrective actions. This is used to evaluate the *need* for a service call and to develop recommendations for the assignment of specific service personnel to service tasks. This approach generally is used in very large and sophisticated service organizations.

"Server" Concepts. Finally, there are three "server" concepts with respect to the implementation of the call-handling and dispatch function.

The "Single Server" Concept. In this approach, the call-handling and dispatch function is carried out by a single individual.

The "Dual Server" Concept. In this approach, the initial call-handling steps are performed by one individual, who is oriented to the customers. Diagnostics and screening, dispatch, assignment, and closing out are done by a second individual, who is oriented to the service force.

"Dual Server" Concept plus Technical Assistance. The third approach involves the "dual server" concept *combined* with a special technical assistance center, which can provide in-depth diagnostics assistance for either customers or field service engineers.

My experience suggests that the best approach initially is to use the *"dual server" concept* for call handling and dispatch. This approach will generally provide the best level of support. It will also allow for changes in the sophistication, size, and structure of the service organization without major and costly changes in call handling.

We will now turn to a discussion of another key function in service: logistics and parts and materials support.

The Logistics and Parts and Materials Support Function

Understanding the improvements in logistics management and control in high-tech equipment service requires a strategic, conceptual approach to the total flow of parts in the field. In the typical service environment, there is a logistics "pipeline" (Fig. 8-3), which involves the continuing flow of parts, materials, subassemblies, and whole units, as well as test equipment, to and from the field. Typically, materials flow into the central warehouse from the organization's manufacturing centers (if they exist), as well as from vendors. They also flow into the central warehouse from the refurbishing center for returned parts. The parts (stockkeeping units), materials, subassemblies, and whole units then flow downward to the regional or district depots and ultimately to service personnel in the field, who use them in performing service tasks for the customer base. Typically, in about 65 to 75 percent of all service tasks, some materials, parts, subassemblies, etc., are utilized.

In general, and typically in maintenance and repair, some stockkeeping units (SKUs) are pulled out of customer equipment and replaced. These include low-cost or nonrepairable items, which are disposed of, and high-cost, repairable items, which are sent back for refurbishment at a central or regional depot. Thus the final link in this integrated, closed-loop pipeline is the refurbishing center, which re-

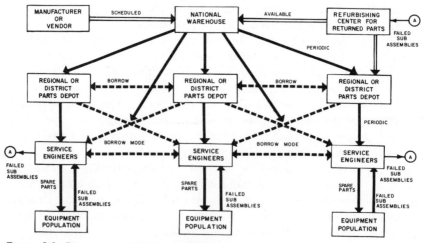

Figure 8-3. Recommended logistics pipeline flow.

turns the units pulled and replaced in the field to the central warehouse or the regional or district depots.

Given this concept of an integrated, closed-loop pipeline, which describes the flow of parts, materials, etc., within the service environment, it is interesting to note some key operational parameters:

1. *Approximately 50 percent of the total value of the inventory within the pipeline is generally found "below" the depots* (i.e., in the field)—in the trunks or hands of the service personnel, or (in some cases) in storage areas at customer sites, or in vehicles traveling to or from the service personnel.

2. *Approximately 80 percent of the total value of the inventory flows from the service engineers and the installed base in the field back into the pipeline through the refurbishing centers each year.*

3. *Approximately 30 to 35 percent of the parts sent by the service engineers to a refurbishing center are, in fact, good units.* This trend is increasing as more and more service engineers use a pull-and-replace philosophy rather than a fix-in-the-field approach as part of their diagnostic test activities in emergency maintenance and repair service. It is important to understand that the pull-and-replace philosophy in the field is dictated by the increasing costs of experienced service engineers and by pressure from customers to reduce repair time. The pull-and-replace approach does allow for the use of less skilled service engineers and reduces the typical mean time for repair; however, it is essential to control the *excessive* use of parts for diagnostic test purposes in the field.

These key parameters all support a general strategic philosophy that the logistics pipeline in field service should be managed as a *totally integrated process*. In addition, one of the most critical points in the pipeline process is the use of parts by service engineers in the field. It is essential to introduce disciplined control through reports on parts usage when it occurs (at the time of completion of the service call). Finally, resupply can best be guaranteed for the service engineers through effective management and control of the refurbishing operations, which can return "used" parts and subassemblies to the pipeline for further use.

Efficient and profitable management and control of logistics support operations in the field also depends on the ability to provide an extremely high fill rate (the rate determined by dividing the number of requests for an SKU into the number of times the request can be filled, at a given stock location) for the service engineer in the field. A high fill rate will minimize the percentage of "broken" or aborted service calls due to lack of parts. This is, of course, not the only parameter of field service, but it is certainly a vitally important one. "Broken" service calls lead to longer service delays and dissatisfied customers. They also lead to inefficient deployment of service staff. Another component of the logistics objective in field service is to minimize the inventory investment and operating costs associated with the logistics pipeline. Investment optimization becomes more critical as the cost of individual SKUs increases. For example, the level of circuit integration and complexity for subassemblies in high-tech electronics is rising daily. This means that the inventory cost of each individual SKU will continue to increase. Thus the need for close control of investment in inventory is more important than ever. Maintaining a very high fill rate for service engineers also depends on close control of investment in inventory, as well as control of the operating costs for logistics support. An optimum range for the fill rate is 85 to 95 percent, depending on the desired level of customer satisfaction (i.e., response and repair time objectives) and willingness to accept investment risk.

Unfortunately, many service organizations still do not operate in accordance with the concept of an integrated logistics pipeline, as described above. Many service executives fail to recognize the need to achieve full control of the logistics pipeline, with emphasis on the tracking of parts used by the service engineers in the field. Other service managers fail to recognize the vital importance of the refurbishment operations. In fact, by using a "just-in-time" approach to central depot repair, it is possible to significantly reduce the total investment in parts. This requires sufficient control over the reporting of parts returns in order to anticipate the flow of SKUs from the field for repair and to estimate accurately the demand for them. These data should then be used to schedule repair operations so that those SKUs which are required can be handled as soon as they are received and then returned to the field as rapidly as possible.

Another problem is that many service organizations are still utilizing inventory control systems originally developed in a manufacturing environment. They fail to recognize that demand patterns for parts in the service environment are much more complex because of the existence of both the SKU return cycle and the long product life cycles, which can materially affect SKU demand patterns over time. In manufacturing, inventory demand is usually forecast on the basis of a production requirements forecast and material requirements planning (MRP) schedules. The parts used in the manufacturing process do not, in effect, "return." In the production environment, the parts and materials flow only outward to the customer. In addition, forecasting needs to be done only during the product production period, not over the full life cycle. The tremendous complexities produced by the integrated, closed-loop pipeline in the typical service environment and the long product life cycles generally invalidate the normal forecast models and mechanisms used in the manufacturing environment for inventory control. Thus it is important to avoid using manufacturing-based forecasting and control models and systems for inventory and logistics support in a service environment.

Controlling the Logistics Pipeline

For service executives in general, and for the managers of parts and materials (logistics) in particular in service organizations, it is vitally important to recognize and understand the key factors that influence the ability to successfully manage and control the logistics pipeline. These factors are as follows:

Density of the Customer Base. This is defined as the number of service customers multiplied by their demand (for service) and divided by a fixed geographic area. For example, if 20 customers each required 1 service action per month in a 1-square-mile area, the customer base would have a greater density $[(20 \times 1) \div 1 = 20]$ than if the same 20 customers were spread over a 10-square-mile area $[(20 \times 1) \div 10 = 2]$. In general, the denser the customer base, the easier it is to define, stock, control, and deliver the materials and parts required for service tasks and to avoid "broken" service calls. A high customer-base density also reduces service delivery time and, therefore, total service response time. Thus, whenever possible, the center of the service operation should be located at the highest concentration of customers.

Since the cost of carrying an inventory of materials and parts in the field generally increases with the size of the customer base, density is also a very critical factor in profitable service performance. Where parts and materials are a significant element of service cost, an increase in the number of customers which does not maintain or improve the customer-base density will result in a lower profit level.

In some cases, customer-base density may not be under the direct control of the service manager. In such cases, the service manager needs to consider expanding the basic service portfolio to meet other service needs of the customer base or allow for different price levels. By expanding the services offered, in terms of either new services or price changes for higher-quality services, it is possible to increase either the customer-base density or revenues. For example, the addition of third-party maintenance service in a product-based service organization can significantly improve customer-base densities and therefore improve the effectiveness of logistics management and control.

Inventory Control. A most important factor affecting the efficiency of logistics management is the level of detail of pipeline control. Parts can be controlled at the individual SKU level or in kits (groups of stock-keeping units to satisfy a specific need); a combination of SKU and kit control is also possible. Both kit control and SKU control have value in logistics management, but it is critical to understand where kit strategies work and do not work. Kits are best employed in situations involving a very low customer-base density or during the introduction or phaseout of a product or service. Kit control is not as effective as SKU control during the growth stage of a product or service life cycle, particularly if the customer-base density is reasonably high. Generally, service organizations should be using a combination of SKU and kit control, down to and including the service person level.

Forecasting Methods and Models.   An additional key to the control of logistics is the use of sophisticated SKU and kit forecasting mechanisms and models, particularly those dealing with sporadic or "spike" demands. A broad array of forecasting mechanisms exists and will be discussed below.

Effective Refurbishment Operations.   The performance of the logistics pipeline can be fine-tuned in high-tech service, where parts or whole units are sent for repair from the field, through the detailed scheduling and control of central or regional refurbishment operations. By performing a quality assurance check when subassemblies arrive from the field and by tracking those subassemblies back to the service engineers who initiated the field service actions, it is possible to identify those service engineers who are overutilizing parts for diagnostic tests. Some service engineers try to fix customer equipment by removing a module and replacing it with a new unit. This is sometimes done without any attempt at diagnostics. If a "good" module is replaced by another, this does not fix the problem; yet a part is utilized. By keeping data on excessive parts usage in the field and by checking for a high rate of "good" return, it is possible to identify service engineers who are engaged in this practice. These service people should be trained to make more effective use of parts and to use more diagnostic procedures in the field.

Also important is the need for detailed scheduling of resupply to the field and very rapid turnaround of repair operations. By using computer-based diagnostics to identify the problems on returned SKUs and automated conveyer systems to move the SKUs to the appropriate work stations for refurbishment, it is possible to bring the total elapsed time from the initiation of a request for repair to shipment to less than 1 day. With this short repair time, a significant percentage of parts requests can be filled from the returns at the refurbishing center rather than from stock at the central warehouse or manufacturing or vendor sources.

Forecasting Methods in Logistics Management and Control

Of the various management techniques available to the service manager for improving the logistics function, one of the most important yet least understood is advanced forecasting to determine the demand for parts and to control inventory levels. Typically, most service organizations use time series data (parts usage and demand over time) and simple averaging to forecast demand. The total parts usage over a given set of time periods is divided by the number of time periods to determine average demand. Unfortunately, such simple linear or averaging techniques do not account for the more complex demand patterns found in a service environment. The demand for parts and materials is primarily affected by both the product or service life cycle and the customer-base density.

Once a product or service has been fully established and its demand is stable, and the density of the customer base is very high, it is relatively easy to forecast demand for parts using simple averages and linear models. Problems in forecasting demand in a service environment occur primarily in situations involving:

The introductory stage of the life cycle

The mature-decline stage of the life cycle

Low customer-base density

For these situations in general and for specific combinations (e.g., low density and introduction of the product or service), the demand for parts is sporadic or "spiked." In these cases, averaging techniques for forecasting demand based on standard or normal time series patterns are often inaccurate.

Examples of SKU demand patterns are shown in Fig. 8-4. One approach to treating the differences in demand patterns is to recognize that the *cumulative* demand pattern is much more stable and predictable than the demand pattern for individual increments of time (Fig. 8-5). The general shape of the cumulative demand curve can be used as a general predictor at various stages of the life cycle. Examples of cumulative demand for a specific stockkeeping unit in the introductory (phase-in) stage, mature-decline (phaseout) stage, and general life cycle (typical) are shown in Fig. 8-6. Inspection of these cumulative curves shows fairly characteristic demand profiles. Exponential or weighted averaging mechanisms, modified by the known characteristics of the life cycle (introduction and phaseout), can then be used to more accurately predict demand on the basis of actual demand data.

Given the cumulative demand data and an explicit identification of the stage in the product life cycle, there are six types of time-series-based forecasting methods which are used in logistics control:

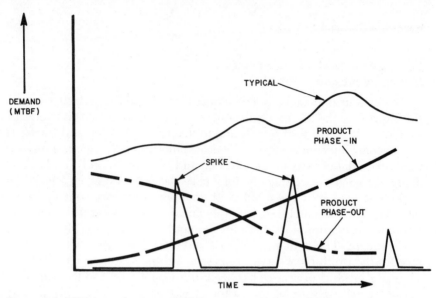

Figure 8-4. SKU demand patterns. (MTBF = mean time between failures.)

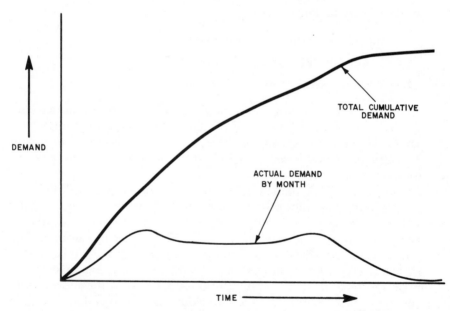

Figure 8-5. General pattern for parts demand.

1. *Simple averaging.* The typical approach used by many unsophisticated service managers is simple averaging. This involves computing the averages of all past demand data in order to determine future demand.

2. *Moving average.* The moving-average method involves selecting

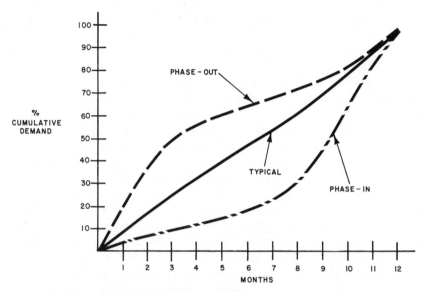

Figure 8-6. Typical demand profiles for active SKUs.

data from just the last few time periods. This provides a somewhat more accurate forecast in response to recent changes and trends.

3. *Weighted moving average.* The weighted-moving-average method involves placing different weights on the previous demand data for different time periods. This approach is, in general, an improvement on the basic moving-average and simple averaging methods, but it does require the introduction of judgments for the weighting mechanisms to be employed in the forecast.

4. *Exponential smoothing.* The exponential smoothing method is a variation of the weighted-moving-average method. It utilizes an exponential weighting curve to develop the weighting mechanisms. Thus the weights are applied systematically, eliminating the need for judgments. Exponential smoothing is probably the most widely used forecasting method among sophisticated logistics managers. However, it does not effectively deal with the difficult introductory, phaseout, and low-density situations that result in spiked demand.

5. *Holt's method.* This is a sophisticated variation of the exponential smoothing approach. It adds factors or historical trends to reflect market knowledge about the stage in the life cycle. In general, Holt's method will improve on exponential smoothing accuracy if the general changes in demand are gradual.

6. *Bayesian inference.* An advanced forecasting method involves the use of Bayesian inference to adjust forecasts on the basis of the proba-

bility of a "state change"* in individual SKUs. Bayesian inference is particularly valid and valuable in the case of slow-moving parts, when demand is spiked or the changes are not gradual. Bayesian inference is based on the assumption that in the service environment, the demand for parts may, in fact, not be equally distributed on the low and high sides but rather will be biased to the "left" or "right" or involve some other unusual characteristic. With Bayesian inference, at least two separate and differentiated formal methods (e.g., exponential smoothing and linear extrapolation) are used to process historical demand data from two or three *previous* time periods in order to forecast demand in the next time period. For the subsequent time period, the new forecast is a weighted average of the results of the two forecasting methods, formed by determining the accuracy of each result on the basis of actual experience. In effect, a weighted index is derived which becomes a new data series that is predicted by means of a third forecasting method. This approach provides for an integrated forecasting model (the original two forecasting methods plus the index) to help logistics managers "learn" about changes in the general characteristics of the demand environment over time. A forecast based on Bayesian inference can be more accurate than forecasts resulting from simple forecasting methods, particularly when demand is spiked or sporadic.

In summary, the demand patterns for high-value, high-cost, repairable stockkeeping units should be forecast by means of exponential smoothing adjusted according to the character of the life cycle (phase-in, phaseout, or typical). Spiked or sporadic demand should be handled through the use of Holt's method or Bayesian inference. Forecasting demand for low-value, low-cost, or disposable items where there is lower cost or less risk for stocking SKUs can be accomplished through exponential smoothing, linear extrapolation, or other standard methods.

Factors Affecting the Use of Forecasting Methods in Logistics Management and Control. The application of an effective forecasting method must start with the recognition of the key factors which influence the demand for stockkeeping units (SKUs). The SKU mix is, of course, dependent upon the service portfolio and support levels offered. If product service and support is included, parts demand will also be affected by the equipment configuration and its level of modularity. Some equipment can include, in one module or subassembly, components which might reflect hundreds of SKUs in another design.

The actual demand patterns for SKUs are affected by:

---

*A "state change" occurs when the demand pattern is disrupted by an unforeseen or abnormal event.

1. The mean time between failures (MTBF) or the reliability of the individual SKU (i.e., how often a part or material is needed)

2. The MTBF and the life cycle of the *parent* product or service

3. The speed of resupply from the next higher stocking level

From the standpoint of the service manager, the speed of resupply can be most directly affected by the service organization. The MTBF or parts and materials demand is, of course, a function of the customer's needs and requirements as well as the equipment design. The life cycle is usually determined by the marketing organization. Both the MTBF and the product life cycle generally cannot be controlled by the service executive. It is therefore essential to make use of as much data as possible about demand and customer service needs in planning for service operations. It is, for example, critical to determine the stage of the life cycle. As shown earlier, products or services can be in an introductory, growth, stabilization, or phaseout stage. The demand for parts will vary dramatically with respect to the life-cycle stage. In the introductory stage, one might find a relatively high demand rate, caused by initial burn-in and/or initial acceptance testing. However, after this initial stage, the stabilization of the product, engineering changes, and other factors tend to reduce the failure rate, and demand becomes stable over a relatively long period of time. As the product begins to mature and/or wear out through use, failure rates begin to edge up. Finally, as the product is pulled back and no longer supported, the demand for parts begins to fall off.

Summary of Steps for Developing and Implementing Forecasting Methods. The first step in developing an effective forecasting approach is to recognize that accurate data must be collected. It is essential to determine the *actual* mean time between failures (MTBF) or demand by stockkeeping unit in order to estimate future demand. The use of data on parts and materials issuance as a surrogate for demand tends to reflect the tendency of service personnel to stockpile parts. Thus issuance data may not be directly related to the life cycle which drives demand, the reliability of the individual parts, or the effects of the actual logistics management strategy employed. The best way to collect true MTBF and demand data is to report on parts and materials use at the time a service call is completed and closed out.

Given that accurate data can be collected on parts and materials demand rates, the next major step, prior to actual forecasting, is to organize the data in a form that allows for analysis on the basis of *cumulative* demand. I have already shown that demand patterns in individual units of time are often masked or are affected by a change in the life cycle.

The general shape of the cumulative demand curve provides significantly more intelligence than the curve for average demand over time. Converting the unit-time demands to cumulative demand smooths out the demand patterns and provides a framework for an analytical consideration of the effects of the life cycle on demand.

The final step is to select and implement the appropriate forecasting method. This involves considering the cost of stocking and the risk or cost penalty to service of running out of stock. The more sophisticated methods (such as Bayesian inference) should be used in high-cost, high-risk situations.

Other Ways to Improve Logistics Control

We have seen that an integrated approach can be used to provide total control over parts and materials used by a service person. There are other techniques which also can be used to improve the efficiency of logistics pipeline management. These approaches are based on improvements to speed the deployment and delivery of parts. Significant improvements in transportation and distribution have led to the recognition that parts can be stored centrally or regionally, with lower inventory at the service engineer level, if *rapid transportation* methods can be used to achieve a high fill rate. Such methods include the use of same-day courier services, parts banks providing same-day delivery, and next-day express service provided, for example, by Federal Express or UPS.

Another approach is the use of a roving van based in each major metropolitan area, which can be dispatched to a service engineer during the day in response to customer calls for assistance. In this approach, each call is initially analyzed through a diagnostics and call-avoidance mechanism in order to identify the parts and materials required for the service task. Computerized systems are then used to determine whether the parts and materials are available in the local stock of the service person to be assigned. If the required items are not available, the roving van, which is usually stocked at the 95 percent level or better, is then dispatched so that the required parts and materials are delivered to the customer's site as soon as, or immediately after, the service engineer arrives. This dynamic use of a roving van with a high stock level (95 to 99 percent), combined with only a midrange investment in service engineer stock for a lower inventory fill rate (say 50 to 60 percent), can produce a significantly higher fill rate for the service engineer.

9

Using Systems and Technology to Improve Service Operations and Productivity

Computerized Service Management Systems

There have been significant developments in the computerized systems and technology for service management and control. These have been due to both the recognition of the major functions involved in the basic operation of the typical service organization and the increasing standardization of the approach to service management and control. The four key functions (see Fig. 9-1) which have been automated are as follows:

- *Call handling and dispatch,* including recording information about the service problem, performing diagnostic screening, providing technical assistance, and, finally, tracking and closing out the service call (see Chap. 8)

- *Logistics and inventory management and control,* including entering and processing orders for parts and materials, tracking and controlling inventory, scheduling and controlling repairs (as discussed in Chap. 8)

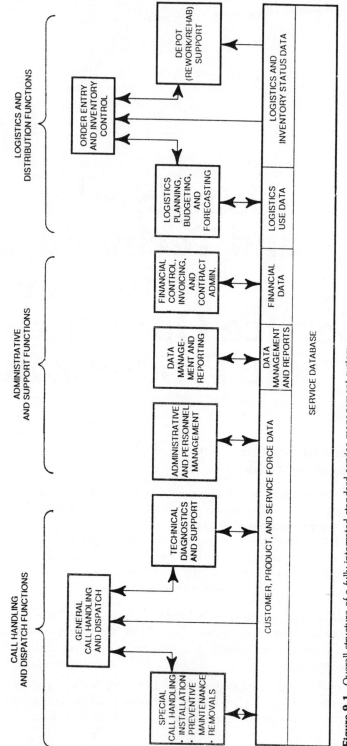

Figure 9-1. Overall structure of a fully integrated standard service management system.

- *Database management,* including standard and ad hoc reporting
- *Financial and administrative management,* including financial control of the revenue and cost components of service operations, such as invoicing, to ensure the receipt of full revenues for services rendered (e.g., warranty and contract services)

These key automated functions can be developed and implemented to provide the service organization with the appropriate framework for managing service operations. The specific operational descriptions provided for each function can be used to establish the preliminary design requirements for a computerized system, or they can serve as a guide for the purchase of standard software from the many vendors of service management systems and technology which currently exist in both the North American markets (see App. B) and the European markets.

The general structure of standard software for service management systems has been influenced by both the growing importance of service within national and international companies and the rapid improvements in computer and communications technology. The typical automated functions which have been developed for service management are discussed below.

Call Handling and Dispatch

For the most part, automated systems today reduce the costs and time involved in performing all the major actions required in call handling and dispatch, from taking a call to closing out the service call. The major actions which can be or have been automated and which exist in standard software packages generally include the following:

- *Taking a call.* This action includes identifying and validating the customer, identifying the specific installed equipment the customer has a problem with, recording the customer's problem statement and other special instructions, and identifying the call taker and the time of the call.

- *Processing the customer's problem statement.* This includes determining service priorities, placing the service request in a schedule queue, using call-avoidance subroutines for possible "phone, or remote, fixes" (such as decision tree analysis, discussed below), routing to a technical analysis center or establishing a callback time, checking for duplicate service calls, etc.

- *Making the service commitment and assignment.* This includes identifying the primary and/or secondary service person to be assigned to the customer, checking the availability and skill levels of service personnel, automatically calculating the estimated time of arrival (ETA) or service completion time, alerting the service person to the service requirement prior to making a service commitment, etc.

- *Dispatching the service person to the customer's location.*   This may be done by means of a telephone; automatic paging to the service person's beeper; or a hand-held, acoustically coupled data terminal or an on-line data communication unit that provides the task assignment, date, and task information. Dispatching may, in many cases, be done during or immediately after the closing out of the previous service call.

- *Tracking the service call.*   This action includes updating the status of the service call for any reason after dispatch. It also includes automatic alerting and escalation if the service call has not been scheduled within a certain time period, or if the service engineer has not arrived on time or has not called in to close out the call or report on the service status within a certain time, or if the customer calls in two or more times about the same problem.

- *Closing out the service call.*   This includes recording the time and parts and materials used on the job, updating the problem codes, recording miscellaneous expenses, identifying emergency parts needed to complete the repair, etc.

Logistics and Inventory Management and Control

Most automated systems provide for the basic logistics and inventory management and control discussed in Chap. 8. In some systems the basic support is extended to include more sophisticated techniques for managing and controlling the full field inventory, including spare parts and materials in the pipeline; the central and regional depots, as well as stock at the service person "trunk" level; and the return cycle, including refurbishment. The major actions generally included in standard logistics software include the following:

- *Inventory tracking and control.*   This affects the entire logistics pipeline (from the central warehouse to the service person's trunk) and involves keeping track of in-transit inventory and returned parts and materials, controlling borrowing, and monitoring the status of stock at the refurbishing center. Data are usually reported on the status of both effective (good) and defective (not good) parts by stockkeeping unit (SKU).

- *Processing of customers' orders for spare parts and materials.*   This action includes on-line entry of orders; order pricing; order tracking and updating; allocation of inventory; automatic backordering as required; generation of picking documents, shipping papers, and transportation documents (e.g., waybills and freight manifests); and the recording of data for future customer billing.

- *Management of customer equipment configuration.* It is important to keep track of the service base of each customer, the source of the base (particularly in the case of third-party maintenance service), and any relocations of the installed base in the field. This action may, in some cases, be incorporated into—and be accessible within—the call-handling and dispatch function to allow for identification of the problem by configuration at the customer's location.

- *Inventory forecasting.* This affects all inventory items and stocking points and is essential for logistics management and for optimizing total inventory levels within the logistics pipeline.

- *Control of refurbishment operations.* This involves scheduling, tracking, and processing parts and materials through the refurbishing center.

- *Inventory replenishment.* This includes automatic generation of requisitions to the next higher inventory stocking level, identification of primary and secondary sources of supply for spare parts and consumables, generation of purchase orders to vendors or replenishment orders to manufacturing facilities, quality control processing, and receipt processing to update inventory records.

- *Inventory maintenance.* This action involves adding and removing inventory (SKU) items, verifying inventory levels through the generation of inventory documents, and automatically updating inventory quantities after physical audits.

- *Vendor performance analysis.* It is always important to analyze the quality, timeliness, and reliability of SKUs provided by vendors.

- *Inventory analysis.* This process includes the identification of obsolete and inactive SKUs, an examination of shipping papers and "where-used" relationships to determine the specific parts that are required to repair specific customer equipment configurations (including model numbers), a review of equipment revision levels within the field, and an evaluation of actual monthly usage of spare parts over the last n months.

Database Management

Automated systems have the capability for both managing a database with a *relational, network,* or *hierarchical* structure and generating online and batch reports (standard reports, as well as special reports on exceptions or critical exceptions). The database should provide, as a minimum:

- A description of customer characteristics, including site installation status
- Service requirements such as failure rate and service demand data
- Service performance data
- Service resources (staff and parts and materials) status

    Typical reports provide information on:

- Call escalation
- Unassigned calls
- Service call history:

    By customer
    By equipment

- Mean time between failures (MTBF)
- Mean time to repair (MTTR)
- Inventory status by location and by SKU
- Open purchase orders
- Revenue and expenses:

    By service operation
    By product line
    By customer

- Customer status:

    Balance owed
    Open and completed service calls
    Contract status
    Installed configuration

- Cost distribution

Financial and Administrative Management

The remaining standard automated function is financial and administrative management, which typically includes the following:

- *Invoicing and billing.* These actions concern the services provided, on either a contract or a time-and-materials basis. Billing involves accumulating costs (time, materials, etc.) and relating them to the service rendered (on a standard contract or time-and-materials basis). Invoicing usually includes the actual generation of the invoice, or bill, and the recording of a customer's liability for the specific or general service rendered.

- *Customer credit checks.* It is essential to validate a customer's credit status for time-and-materials or contract service calls.

- *Management of accounts receivable and accounts payable.* This action involves updating accounts receivable data and making payments to vendors and other suppliers of consumables and services that support the field sales and service.

- *Cost allocation.* Direct and indirect expenses are allocated to accurately reflect the profitability of the local service organization by customer, service area, service engineer, or some other criterion.

- *Cash collection and handling.* Cash receipts are applied to accounts receivable generated by time-and-materials service calls or contract maintenance billing.

- *Profit analysis.* This is done to determine the contributions to profitability by specific service call, service area, service engineer, customer, type of equipment being maintained, maintenance contract, or any combination of these elements.

Summary of Functional Computerized Service Management Capabilities

On the basis of an analysis of field service management needs and requirements and an evaluation of the current state-of-the-art computerized systems and technology to support the field service operations through the 1990s, I recommend the development and implementation of a *service management system*, as structured in Fig. 9-1. The integrated, centralized service management system should support the functions of call handling and dispatch, logistics and inventory management and control, database management, and financial and administrative management. The system should be implemented in a functional, *modular* form utilizing *executive control*. This should allow for the addition of advanced options when major changes are required for the system. As the database stabilizes and service management experience increases, other advanced features can be added.

The service management system should be physically based at the service organization's headquarters, with distributed capabilities for on-line interactive access from each of the major regional and/or district offices, logistics depots (central and regional), and field stocking points.

The computerized service management system should be able to integrate and interface with other existing management systems, such as companywide accounting, financial, and reporting systems or billing and invoicing systems.

Technology for Improving Communications

The growing demand for improved efficiency and productivity in service has also created the need for new technology for tying headquarters-oriented service management systems to the service staff in the field (e.g., electronics-based communications and technology for processing, storing, and retrieving data). The feasibility of having service people in the field who are fully trained in the tremendously complex service diagnostics and repair procedures and have the capacity to both *remember* and *apply* these procedures is rapidly being challenged by the growing variety of service options. In addition, the service technician's task is constantly changing and evolving because of the increased reliability and growing modularity of parts, as well as the increasing tendency to utilize built-in service capability. The key, therefore, to improving the productivity, efficiency, and effectiveness of the service people or technicians in the field is to provide them with improved communications and access to a growing variety of data on an on-line, real-time basis.

In broad terms, five new technologies have been developed and implemented to increase communications and reporting in the field:

1. *Beeping and paging units.* Beeping and paging systems, operating on a local, regional, or national level, can provide a direct alert to the service person from a central call-handling and dispatch location.

2. *Hand-held, acoustically coupled data terminals.* Another technology developed to improve service force productivity in the field is the hand-held data terminal, providing acoustically coupled capability for data downloading and uploading. The units are specifically designed for service use and provide the capability to directly receive calls for service and close out service actions, as well as request parts and technical assistance.

3. *On-line, real-time data communication units.* A new class of computer technology has been developed and tested to improve field service communications. This usually involves a highly reliable FM or cellular radio that provides a direct link between a central service headquarters and a service person in the field. The hand-held data communication unit usually also contains a computer device and pro-

vides the capability for linking the service engineer with a central or regional service headquarters so that information on assigned service calls can be directly communicated to the service person; thus the service person can close out existing calls, report on the use of parts, request new parts and materials, and obtain diagnostic test information. The major advantage is the elimination of the need to use a local telephone or require access to the public telephone networks.

4. *Lap-top and portable computer systems with embedded diagnostic capabilities.* Significant new developments in portable and lap-top computers make it possible to provide advanced capabilities directly to the service engineer in the field for diagnostic tests and evaluation. These computer units typically provide embedded diagnostic capabilities for supporting tests and problem identification and evaluation. Field units have recently come into use which provide advanced diagnostic capabilities utilizing artificial intelligence for self-learning.

5. *Hand-held information storage and retrieval systems.* Very recent technological innovations are portable, high-capacity storage and retrieval systems that use high-density videotape and provide on-line displays with on-board digital computer capabilities. These systems, now under development, provide the service person in the field with an electronically based "service manual" that allows for random-access search and retrieval.

In summary, technology has already been developed, or is currently being developed and implemented, which can significantly improve the efficiency and effectiveness of communication from a central or regional service management system to a service engineer in the field. Communication is facilitated in an on-line, real-time mode through an FM radio or a cellular radio; it is also provided directly through hand-held storage and retrieval systems or acoustically coupled terminals.

Artificial Intelligence and Advanced Diagnostics

The rapidly escalating cost of labor and parts inventories in service operations has led to the need for new technology to improve the efficiency of service. Service call productivity can be improved in three ways:

1. *By reducing actual service requirements* through effective problem diagnosis *prior* to dispatch. This includes the use of self-help, preventive maintenance, and other call-avoidance mechanisms.
2. By using improved problem diagnostics to *optimize the actual re-*

quired service calls. This includes identifying the required service resource skill levels and delivering the required parts and materials.

3. *By reducing on-site and depot repair time* through more rapid isolation and diagnosis of the actual problem in the field and the full use of previous service call history and data.

All three approaches depend upon improved and more efficient problem identification and diagnostics. Artificial intelligence (AI) technology—computerized mechanisms for decision support—can help in improving the quality, efficiency, and effectiveness of problem diagnostics. The potential improvements can be evaluated by examining field experience.

My analysis of the statistics of service operations shows that a very significant percentage (up to 50 percent) of the calls for service from customers in high-tech environments do not actually require on-site service (see Table 9-1). This is due to a variety of reasons, including the following:

1. *The problem is caused by the user's failure to follow certain procedures.* Instructing the customer in the right procedures by phone will correct the problem as viewed by the customer.

2. *The problem, as initially reported by the customer, is due to external causes and will correct itself shortly.* The customer simply needs to be assured that this will occur. Also, the customer should be given a reasonably accurate estimate of when the correction will occur.

3. *The problem is due to a software error or an operationally related issue,* which can be corrected directly by the user, without assistance from the service force.

4. *The problem is very minor, requiring a simple adjustment or some other corrective action which can be performed by the user directly,* if the user is willing to take the action, or with the provision of a part or a consumable item which is available at the customer's site or can be sent directly to the site.

My research shows that if problems are accurately identified and diagnosed at the time the customers call, approximately 35 to 50 percent of all service requests will not require on-site assistance. Some problems can be corrected via a telephonic exchange of information between the customer and the service organization or by shipment of a part or a consumable item to the customer's site. Since a typical on-site service call requires approximately 20 to 40 minutes for service engineer travel time and approximately 30 minutes to an hour or more for the on-site repair, the service time commitment is generally a *minimum* of 1 to 2

Table 9-1. Typical Requirements for Handling Customers' Problems
(The Numbers Are Percentages of the Total Calls for Service That Are Received)

Disposition of problem	Data processing systems	Types of equipment serviced		Medical electronics
		Terminals and peripheral equipment	Telecommunications equipment	
Requires on-site repair:	60	65	50	60
Requires parts and technical skills	65	75	50	65
Requires technical skills only	35	25	50	35
Can be corrected remotely:	40	35	50	40
Problem self-corrects	5	5	50*	15
Problem is due to operator's failure to follow procedures	25	20	20	35
Operator can correct software or procedure error	45	40	20	20
Operator can make an adjustment or perform some other corrective action	25	35	10	30
Total	100	100	100	100

*Including network-related correction or repair.
SOURCE: D. F. Blumberg & Associates analysis of data from 20 companies for selected months in 1980.

hours for a simple repair and up to 8 hours or more for complex problems. On the basis of approximately $44,000 a year as the average cost of direct compensation, benefits, and direct overhead to support a service person in the field, and a 220-day work year, the average direct hourly cost per service person is approximately $25. Thus each service call (involving an *average* time commitment of 4 hours) that is avoided results in a measurable productivity improvement which can be valued, on the average, at $100. If a typical service organization, handling an average of 1000 requests for service a day, can reduce the number of service calls by 30 percent or more through the use of artificial intelligence for problem diagnostics, it can realize a *direct cost savings* of $30,000 a day, or $6 million per year. This is a very significant incentive to consider artificial intelligence and related call-avoidance diagnostics as a productivity improvement mechanism.

While I have used examples in a high-tech environment to establish the concept of diagnostics and call avoidance, it is important to recognize that this has broader applications. Many service issues in a bank or an airline reservations operation, for example, often result from a customer's lack of familiarity with procedures or practices. The use of technology to help customers understand procedures can help to improve service responsiveness and customer satisfaction. In a retail store, systems and procedures which can help a customer find the right product or service rapidly, without requiring waiting for a salesclerk, can help to improve service performance and delivery. Thus the first step toward applying new technology for improving service productivity is to determine if situations exist in which less than complete on-site service needs to be provided to meet customer needs and requirements. If this is the case, we then need to define and describe those types of service situations and develop the means to recognize when such situations exist.

The second step is to evaluate the willingness of customers to accept less than complete service. Important to this analysis is the need to understand and accept the increasing trend toward customer acceptance of service alternatives. Numerous surveys of the requirements for service and support show the willingness of customers to accept service alternatives, particularly if they can be provided with clear choices as to more or less service at higher or lower costs. Users recognize that there are a number of different channels for the delivery of service that can be used individually or in some combination:

- Technical assistance can be provided via telephone.

- Technical assistance and repairs can be provided at the customer's site.

Table 9-2. Attitudes of Respondents toward Effectiveness of Methods for Service Delivery

(Attitudes Expressed as Percentages of Respondents)

Service delivery mechanism	Percentage of problems which can be handled by delivery mechanism		
	25% or less	25% to 75%	75% or more
Telephone diagnostics	30	40	30
On-site repair	20	60	20
Delivery of parts and/or consumable supplies	40	55	5
Instruction manuals and training in self-repair	70	25	5

SOURCE: D. F. Blumberg & Associates surveys in computer, office automation, telecommunications, building automation, and process control markets, 1983–1988.

- Parts and/or consumable supplies can be delivered to the customer's site.
- Experience and technical knowledge can be delivered through training and user documentation.

A surprisingly high percentage of respondents indicated that a significant number of problems could be solved directly via telephone diagnostics (see Table 9-2). The trend over the last decade has been a continual increase in the positive attitude of users toward the process of self-repair, if *on-line dynamic direction* is also available as to what to do via telephone. A user does want and need the positive reinforcement (by phone) of the validity of the self-service action, along with continuing assurance from the service organization that if the "self-fix" does not work, a service person will be dispatched.

Mechanisms for Remote Diagnostics and Repair

Three basic approaches can be used in a service environment to support and provide (remote) diagnostics in order to minimize the number of on-site service calls. They involve technical assistance centers, decision analysis, and embedded diagnostics. Artificial intelligence technology can be used to implement each approach.

Technical Assistance Centers. The simplest approach is to set up a technical assistance center (TAC) which can be called up directly by a customer (or service representative) or provided as part of a standard call-handling procedure. The TAC is normally staffed by experienced service personnel who are supported by extensive documentation and test technology. Typically, a TAC is organized by product or product group. Customer calls for assistance are picked up by an individual TAC specialist, who proceeds to handle the customer call, using personal experience, knowledge and skills, and past events to advise on actions to take. TAC specialists can complete a call directly or request further action, resulting in the subsequent dispatch of a service person to the field if necessary or the shipment of a part or a consumable item to provide the needed service for the customer.

Diagnostic Decision Analysis through Artificial Intelligence. A more sophisticated approach to diagnosing problems involves the use of decision tree analysis and evaluation. Decision analysis techniques can be used to determine service requirements in two types of situations:

1. *Mature, older* service situations for which a reasonable historical database exists relating problems and symptoms observed to causes and corrective actions

2. *New or recently introduced* situations which have been subjected to a quantitative failure analysis and reliability evaluation

An example of a basic tree structure used in service is shown in Fig. 9-2. It provides a logical progression through "treelike" branches from an initial "complaint" provided by a customer because of the failure of a "machine" or piece of equipment, to the identification of "symptoms,"

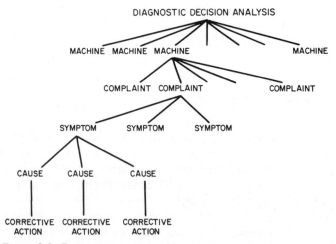

Figure 9-2. Basic tree structure for diagnostic decision analysis.

to the determination of "causes" and "corrective actions." This approach does not, of course, have to be limited to a machine or equipment problem. Any problem can be defined in terms of a decision tree structure within a sequence as follows:

- *Broad problem* area
- *Symptoms or requirements* related to the service issue or problem
- *Causes or characteristics* of the service requirement, defined by the symptoms
- *Service action* to be taken on the basis of the causes, characteristics, or symptoms identified

For example, in a bank, the same approach could be used to identify the need for a currency transfer in an international trade situation. In this case, we would need to identify the problem (an international trade transaction), the related requirement (translate U.S. dollars into British pounds sterling), the specific characteristics of the transaction (convert US$20 to £12.5), and, finally, the service action (transfer $20 from customer account 1526 in New York as £12.5 to customer account 3173 in London). Similar steps could be developed for a service situation in an airline or a retail establishment. The basic procedure involves breaking down the diagnostic decision into its component elements and dealing with them in one of two ways:

- In a step-by-step sequence from higher level to lower level on the basis of "expert" experience (*rules-based decision*)
- According to the interrelationship between causes and effects (*model-based decision*)

We can use formal, computer-aided (through artificial intelligence) decision analysis to help improve the service process at a number of stages, including the following:

- *The initial stage of the call-handling function*—to more rapidly identify the problem
- *The technical diagnostics stage*—to more accurately indicate the symptoms and causes
- *The dispatch stage*—to optimize the response on the basis of a more accurate identification of the required service action

Embedded Diagnostics. A third approach for problem diagnostics involves the creation of formal "triggering" mechanisms that automatically generate a defined service request. In a high-tech environment, this means building diagnostic test and evaluation technology directly into the equipment. This technology automatically senses problems and reports them directly to a central monitoring center, defining each problem and the associated symptoms, probable cause(s), and recommended corrective action.

This embedded diagnostics capability can also identify potential problems before they are observed by the user and thereby support the identification of preventive maintenance actions. Several computer manufacturers—including IBM, Honeywell, Control Data, and Amdahl—and major copier firms such as Xerox have included a remote diagnostics capability in their product or system designs, providing a direct, on-line, interactive capability for maintenance and repair.

AT&T, for example, implemented an extremely sophisticated remote diagnostics capability for its Dimension PBX telecommunications equipment, as well as for standard telephone sets and equipment. AT&T and other companies have found that hardware design employing embedded diagnostics can reduce on-site service calls by as much as 50 percent.

Applications of Artificial Intelligence and Advanced Diagnostics

In broad terms, artificial intelligence and advanced diagnostics have two types of applications in the service environment: in *expert systems* and *self-organizing or statistical decision systems*.

- *Expert systems.* Expert systems provide a framework for gathering and organizing the experience of "expert" service engineers, usually on the basis of ex ante (i.e., before-the-fact) evaluation. This is usually called heuristic analysis. Two types of expert systems are in use:

  Rules-based expert systems. These are produced by recording and linking the heuristic decisions which are made by the human mind when solving problems or troubleshooting a unit or systems fault. A rules-based expert system literally documents and logically organizes the individual and discrete steps which a service specialist must go through to remedy a fault or provide service. Typically, it is structured to work in a forward-chaining or backward-chaining format, depending upon the specific problem it was designed to solve.

  Model-based expert systems. These are developed from a prioritized database of the system's or unit's calculated or anticipated failure structure and behavior. This format makes the model-based approach better suited for the fault analysis of new equipment which service personnel may not be familiar with; methods to add historical information automatically as it is developed are desirable in a model-based expert system.

Generally, these types of systems employ the software-hardware combination of a development "engine," inference "engine," and knowledge base.

- *Self-organizing or statistical decision systems.* Self-organizing systems provide the capability to organize incoming failure data on the basis of statistically relevant events or trends. This occurs in a self-reinforcing format with each new data item used to temper the decision process for the next "round." Examples of self-organizing systems include, but are not limited to, the following:

  Decision tree analysis. The decision process is structured in a statistically sensitive "trunk, branch, and leaf" hierarchy. This concept is most easily described in terms of a top-to-bottom tree diagram linking *problem* to *symptoms*, symptoms to *causes*, and causes to recommended and actual *corrective actions*.

  Parallel analysis. New data structures are created on the basis of the statistical validation of occurrence of individual failures. The probability or risk of individual events is computed and displayed for each step in the diagnostic process.

  Nonformatted analysis. A combination of symbolic (graphic) and logical relations is used to relate failures or service needs in an "if-then" sequence. Usually, the nonformatted analysis makes use of "pictures" to logically relate a service requirement to a particular cause.

There is also a third concept, still in the development stage: a process-model expert system. The process-model expert system is based not on a prioritized database for a specific product or system but rather on a general model of the troubleshooting process that would be conducted by a human expert. The primary advantages of such an approach over the expert system or self-organizing system are as follows:

It is applicable to any service situation, since the inference "engine" is not bound to a specific data structure.

The knowledge base can be created by a product or technical specialist without the requirement of a "knowledge" engineer or programming skills.

Since it is not "hardwired" to either a system "expert" or a specifically structured knowledge base, the database, including variant configurations, can be easily modified and updated as new information is received and processed.

This broad AI technology is being implemented and applied in the field or depot service environment in three forms:

1. *Centralized batch and off-line technology* for the analysis and evaluation of trends and for the development of decision rules and models at a central location

2. *Centralized on-line systems* used in an automatic mode at a central location

3. *Portable technology* to provide decision support capability in the field or for local depot tests; for use by the service engineer directly, in a decentralized (i.e., field) location

All three are in various stages of development and application. My initial evaluation strongly suggests that both the centralized on-line and portable systems can significantly improve the productivity and efficiency of service operations.

Related to the new technology for diagnostics and artificial intelligence are new developments in portable and lap-top computers and other types of data communications technology. These new developments allow advanced diagnostics and AI mechanisms to be carried directly by the service personnel into the field, and they significantly improve the ability to communicate directly from and to the field site. (Data communications technology is described earlier in this chapter.)

The Benefits of Artificial Intelligence and Advanced Diagnostics

Remote diagnostics and artificial intelligence technology is increasingly being applied in three broad but related service markets:

1. Data processing and office automation systems

2. Network systems (both voice and data)

3. Building automation and heating, ventilation, and air-conditioning (HVAC) control

Examples of service organizations now successfully employing advanced diagnostics technology are Texas Instruments; Digital Equipment Corporation (DEC); Honeywell, Inc.; Bull; AT&T; and Carrier. These organizations and others have generally found that investment in new AI technology can generally be repaid in approximately 1 to 2 years. For very large organizations, the repayment could be made in less than 6 months.

Texas Instruments, for example, has successfully applied Personal Consultant, its internally developed artificial intelligence system, to improve the efficiency of depot-level board diagnostics and repair, and Honeywell is now developing an advanced system to improve call dispatch and assignment. Honeywell has also been successfully using its Mentor system and lap-top technology for field repair of chillers and related HVAC equipment. DEC has been using remote diagnostics for servicing networks and mainframe computers.

Clearly, there are *advantages* in using the new artificial intelligence technology, including:

- Reduced service response and repair time
- Reduced parts inventories
- Reduced need for in-depth and costly human diagnosis
- Reduced service staff to achieve a given service performance level
- Increased confidence in systems and technology for "automatic" problem resolution

However, the AI technology does also generate some disadvantages:

- Requirement of a significant investment in data collection, processing, and delivery technology
- Increased dependence on technology for fault identification and isolation, thus reducing the need for and use of the creative, heuristic human capability for problem identification and resolution
- Reduced reliance on experienced service engineers, ultimately impacting the need for a "personal touch" in the service control specifications and in the data bank

Here is an example of the economic advantages of AI use. In a service organization with approximately 200 engineers and annual service revenues of $30 million (i.e., $150,000 per service engineer), the application of advanced diagnostics and artificial intelligence could produce the following benefits:

- Reduced on-site service calls (call-avoidance rate of 15 percent)

- Reduced repeat calls by service engineers, due to lack of parts or skills (50 percent reduction in "broken" or repeat calls)

- Improved field repair time (35 percent reduction in mean time to repair)

- Reduced training time (20 percent reduction in service engineer training time)

- Reduced inventory carrying costs (25 percent reduction in parts inventory levels in the field)

These improvements could result in a direct, measurable savings of $3.6 million annually, or 12 percent of revenues. The planned investment of approximately $3 million in diagnostics and AI technology, including a $7000 portable unit for each service engineer, could then be returned in approximately 1 to 2 years.

Pragmatic experience also indicates that a highly applicable and transferable technology can be developed for call handling and dispatch. The self-organizing technology appears to be most transferable and useful. When this technology is part of a fully integrated field service management system incorporating both call handling and logistics control, the capture of data and the use of the data in field- and depot-based diagnostics are best achieved. My overall evaluation indicates that remote diagnostics and artificial intelligence will continue to be used in the service industry. The payoff will increase as more standard, off-the-shelf technology becomes available that is designed specifically for tests and repairs in the field and depot service environment.

Factors Influencing Changes in Service Management and Control

The very significant changes that have been taking place in the growth of the service industry over the last 10 years have, in turn, led to dramatic improvements in the strategic management, control, and direction of call handling and logistics and parts support. These changes have been, to a large degree, initiated by a new emphasis on the management of service. From the 1950s through the 1970s, in almost all industrial market sectors, *service* was generally viewed and operated as a *cost* center. Typically, the service organizations were highly decentralized, focusing primarily on the tactical, short-term issue of assigning the service person. Service management, to the extent it existed, was primarily concerned with the *supervisory* questions associated with field control of service personnel, and heavy emphasis was placed on achieving general customer satisfaction within the budget or cost allocation. In this framework, logistics and parts and materials support generally came from the "factory" or manufacturing function. Parts were usually obtained from the manufacturing inventory or, in crisis situations, directly from the production line.

This highly decentralized, cost-center approach to service changed dramatically in the 1980s and will continue to evolve through the 1990s (see Table 9-3). Service is now typically being managed as a profit center or an independent line of business; it is generally run centrally, with its own logistics support and parts management and control function. In

Table 9-3. Trends in Service Organization Operating Structure, 1970–2000

Key aspects of operations	Time frame		
	1970–1979	1980–1989	1990–2000
Type of financial structure	Cost center	Profit center under marketing or independent line of business	Independent, strategic line of business
Organizational form	Highly decentralized	Centralized or regional	Highly centralized
Logistics and inventory control	Decentralized, under manufacturing	Decentralized, under service	Centralized, under service
Use of call avoidance, artificial intelligence, and remote diagnostics	Not used	Experimental	Extensive use
Use of integrated management systems	Very limited	Extensive use in larger firms, primarily in high-tech (EDP/OA)* markets	Extensive use across all markets
Use of field data systems	Not used	Use of acoustically coupled call-in devices Limited use of on-line technology using FM or cellular radio	Extensive use

*EDP/OA = electronic data processing and office automation.

the modern service organization, a customer's call for service is increasingly handled by determining the actions that are required in order to resolve the customer's problems in the most timely and cost-effective manner possible rather than by automatically dispatching a service person. In-depth technical analysis, remote diagnostics, and call-avoidance mechanisms are now being used increasingly as an on-line part of the call-handling function to avoid, altogether, the need for on-site service calls. (For example, customers can be advised to take their own corrective actions, or parts, supplies, corrective software, etc., can be dispatched.) In those cases in which an actual on-site call is required, after call-avoidance diagnostics, the call-handling function provides specific recommendations as to which parts the service engineers should take with them on the service call, thus reducing the percentage of "broken" calls due to the lack of parts or technical assistance. The improvements in call handling and dispatch have been coupled with improvements in the control of logistics.

In summary, integrated service management systems and technology linked to the service engineers in the field will continue to improve the efficiency of service operations. Changes in systems and technology will support the long-term trend toward centralized management and control of service as a full line of business.

Development of Advanced Systems for Service Management and Control

Once the full service strategy and staffing plan have been developed, it is then essential to design, develop, and implement the management systems and controls to coordinate service delivery and efficiently capture the data so vital to both the day-to-day and long-term direction of the service operation.

The first step is to specify the required functionality and systems environment on the basis of the size, structure, and dimensions of the service organization. An audit of existing operations should be carried out to identify:

- Current practices and procedures, systems, and operating approach
- The cost of operating and supporting each major function in the service organization (call handling and dispatch, logistics and inventory support, database management, etc.)
- Opportunities for productivity improvement and cost reductions

In the absence of any corporate constraints, the systems environment should generally make use of fourth-generation language and a relational or networked database management system. The very extensive use of data in a service management system requires powerful capabilities for the storage and retrieval of data and the ability to extract and organize the data on a dynamic basis to produce reports. Of course, the systems environment may also be affected by the hardware and software that are available and by the need to integrate the service management systems with other general systems of the corporate organization.

The final description and definition of the required support functions—i.e., the general system concept for the handling of calls and logistics support, and the communications and data systems (hardware and utility and database software)—must then be specified. This specification should be evaluated to determine:

- Alternatives for development and implementation, including:

  Internal development
  Internal development with external design, consultation, and contract
    programming assistance
  Use of purchased systems and software

- The cost, time requirements, and risk associated with each alternative
- The best choice, based on a cost-benefit analysis and evaluation

With the increasing availability of standard service management system software, the options for internal development for all but the largest organizations requiring highly specialized functions are becoming increasingly expensive. More than 20 vendors of service management systems now offer service management system packages covering all the major functions discussed earlier in this chapter; the software packages are offered with a wide variety of data processing platforms and programming languages. A recent survey of available software is presented in App. B.

In general, implementing these service management systems will require an investment of $25,000 to $100,000 in software and an equivalent amount in hardware. However, experience suggests that these investments can be repaid in less than 2 years after implementation.

A preliminary functional specification should be prepared as a basis for proposals for both a shortlist of service management system vendors and an internal MIS (management information system) development staff. The best candidates should be chosen on the basis of (1) the ability to meet the stated functional requirements, (2) the cost of the system, (3) the elapsed time for development and implementation, (4) the level of support offered by the vendor, and (5) the risks associated with the development effort.

Final selection of the service management system vendor(s) will then lead to implementation. The implementation effort must include:

- Conversion of data
- Training of the staff using the system in the key functions of the system
- Training of the support staff
- Development of procedures and practices for using the system and training of the field service engineers in these new procedures and their interface with the system

A critical step in the implementation process is to deal with *both* the computerized systems and the related operating (manual) procedures and practices. It is also important to select and implement a system which is modular and flexible, to allow for changes in the service environment and the introduction of new technology over time.

The final step in implementation is to effect a formal review to determine the fit of the delivered system to the preliminary functional specification. In fact, a review of both system functions and features and any new opportunities for improvement should be conducted at least once a year. This will ensure that the emerging needs and requirements of the service organization will be met with state-of-the-art systems.

In summary, the development and implementation of advanced systems to improve service operations involve the following steps:

1. Specifying the required functionality and systems environment on the basis of the needs of the service organization.

2. Specifying the support functions: the call-handling and logistics support concept and the communications and data processing needs. (This step includes the identification and evaluation of development options.)

3. Establishing a vendor shortlist and an internal MIS development option on the basis of criteria such as ability to satisfy functional requirements.

4. Selecting the vendor(s) and implementing the systems. (This step includes a continuing review of system performance.)

10

Summary: The Emerging Role of Strategic Service

In many high-tech companies in today's economy, a basic scenario is being played out which has a direct bearing on the value of a strategic service approach. Typically, in these companies, one or several business lines have begun to mature or have already reached the mature stage of the life cycle. Product sales are no longer growing, and profit margins are eroding. On the other hand, for these products, the installed base has become significantly large, and therefore, the revenues and profit margins from service have become substantial relative to the revenues and profits from the basic *product* business. In these situations, service sales continue to grow (because of the increasing installed base requiring services), while product sales are stabilized or declining.

As the senior managers of these companies begin to deal with the changing fortunes of their product lines and product portfolios, a typical first reaction is to attempt to offset declining product revenues and profits by reducing costs in the product business arena and in the one area which has demonstrated profit margins: the service business. The typical result of this initial top management reaction is increased pressure on the service manager or executive to continue to maintain or, in fact, increase service quality and performance while at the same time holding or even cutting service budgets and the related service staffs. This extremely difficult dilemma of *both* maintaining or improving service quality and reducing service operating costs must be resolved by either top management or the senior service executive. A possible resolution of this extremely difficult conflict is to attempt to move to *strategic service*: the management of service as an independent line of business, one that is operated as a strategic unit in parallel with product lines rather than as a cost or contribution center in tactical support of an already existing product line or product portfolio. The best choice with respect to the direction of service in high-tech markets is clearly strategic. The service executive must recognize and understand that it is possible *only in the short run* to maintain service quality while at the same time reducing the service budget and staff. Clearly, in the long run, such an approach will cause service quality to suffer. The deterioration of service quality and performance will then lead to an ever-increasing loss of market share and drop in product sales. A basic issue facing the service manager is how to efficiently and effectively sell top management on the need to view service as a strategic line of business. The real question for the top executive is how to best implement the strategic service approach.

Selling Top Management on Strategic Service

It is most important, in selling top management on strategic service, to provide an understanding of the basic concept of service as a separate line of business and to develop an understanding of how service and product are both similar and different in terms of management and financial control. I have shown that strategic service, as a *separate and independent line of business*, provides three key values to the corporation:

1. It is possible to increase product sales and add value to products through the provision of installation and warranty services.

2. Revenues and profits can be generated directly from continuing maintenance and repair services and related support services.

3. Strategic service is a mechanism for general market control.

Steps in Developing the Strategic Service Approach

The steps in developing a strategic view of the value of service are based upon the development of quantitative internal data relating to service revenues, profit margins, and costs, as well as external data relating to changing customer and market requirements and needs for service. The first step is the construction of an economic model for service as a stand-alone business. A critical part of this construction is identifying and appropriately allocating the full revenues associated with the costs of service operations. These attempts at allocation could create significant difficulties in terms of fully recognizing service revenues and profits as compared with product revenues and profits. Typically, in most cost-based service operations, installation, warranty, training services, parts, and other cost-generating elements relating to the initial sale are often provided for the product division or group on a "free" or direct cost basis only. An interdivisional transfer price must be designed to reflect not only the direct cost but also the overhead cost of service (for the standby ability to serve within a given time frame); the transfer price must reflect every line-item cost of service delivered to either the product division or the end user. This is essential in order to examine the true revenues and profitability of service.

This analysis will usually show that under a fully allocated profit and loss model with interdivisional transfer pricing of services at market value, the service organization is typically quite profitable, whereas the product businesses (which had previously appeared to be profitable) operate in a marginal or loss situation. A considerable amount of "apparent profit" in product operations is actually generated by providing the "customer-required services" at lower than market cost. While the product organizations might well argue that some portion of these revenues is generated as a by-product of product sales, a true analysis must be based upon an examination of a full profit and loss statement for service. The "credit" for the sales pulled through by service can be reflected in a set interdivisional transfer price or a set sales commission. However, the lack of any type of full revenue and profit analysis of the service operation will tend to lead to false conclusions concerning the relative profitability of the product sales versus service sales activity.

After the construction of an economic model for the analysis of the service operations, the next step is to carry out appropriate market studies in order to identify:

1. The size of the present customer base of the firm or the future customer base target
2. The changing service requirements and needs of the users in the customer base
3. The cross elasticity of demand between products and services as viewed by the customer
4. The service price elasticity of demand as a function of service requirements, needs, and quality

In general, market studies of this type will clearly identify an increasing interest of the customer base in a single service vendor who can offer a single-point-of-contact, integrated service approach. This is particularly true for customers who have a high value in use for service. The purpose of the market research is to define and describe the market for services. The market research will generally show the existence of a large or increasing segment of the customer population interested in a single-point-of-contact service manager and integrated service offerings. To the extent that a high degree of product-service cross elasticity of demand and a significant segment of price-inelastic and price-linear customers exist, the demand for products can also be improved through a strategic service orientation. The arguments for establishing service as a *separate, strategic line of business* become strongest where the service price elasticity of demand is low (demand is inelastic or linear) and where product-service cross elasticity of demand is high, or service-biased.

In summary, operating service as a strategic line of business requires (1) a careful *internal financial analysis* based upon an economic model which provides a full allocation of revenues against costs, using market-based interdivisional transfer pricing, (2) *market research* to clearly define product-service cross elasticity of demand, service price elasticity of demand, and the changing service requirements and needs of the customer base, and (3) a *combined evaluation* which balances the three key goals of strategically directed service:

1. *Providing support for the existing high-tech product business* in terms of maintaining or improving customer satisfaction levels

2. *Developing revenues and profits from the sale of service* to meet the emerging customer requirements and needs for service independently of the product business

3. *Providing broader service capability* to meet the total service needs and requirements of the customers, particularly where emerging requirements exist for integrated, single-point-of-contact service

While the concept of the provision of service independently of the product business was difficult to accept a few years ago, there is a growing recognition of the fact that increasingly standard technology found in the marketplace, coupled with the general tendency toward the integration of high-tech products into one common system, has already created a real customer requirement for integrated service. Responding to this requirement can generate service revenue as well as product revenue.

Future Directions of Service

It is critically important for service executives and managers to look into the future and prepare for the shock of change. Service has undergone a major transformation and will continue to change. At the start of the 1970s, service was run primarily on a decentralized, cost-center basis, reporting through either manufacturing or marketing and distribution, to support the basic product lines of the company. While the very large companies, such as Xerox, IBM, and Texas Instruments, were developing customized systems for call handling and logistics control, the majority of the service organizations operated their systems and procedures on a manual or, at best, semiautomated batch basis. Independent, or third-party, maintenance service was still in its infancy; it was regarded as a cheap, low-quality alternative to the high-performance manufacturers' service organizations.

The mid- to late 1980s saw significant market, competitive, and technological developments in service management leading to a major recognition of service as a vital, growing business center with the concurrent shift toward operating service on a profit and loss basis. In fact, there has been growing recognition of the strategic value of service as a line of business. The most profound changes, however, have been in service organization structure and the application of computer systems and technology. Many service organizations have made the transition from highly decentralized, fragmented operations toward regional or centralized businesses utilizing on-line systems for call handling and dispatch and logistics control. While these general trends toward centralization, the operation and management of service as a full profit center, and the application of computerized technology in service management will certainly continue in the 1990s, it is equally clear that in this decade, service managers and top corporate executives will have to deal strategically with major changes if the service organization is to not only survive but also grow in stature and profitability.

Key Structural Changes in the 1990s

Major changes will be created in the 1990s as a result of the increasing reliability and maintainability of products. The trends of the 1980s—the proliferation of technology, the increasing dependence of the users on that technology for day-to-day operations, increased networking, and the increase in customer requirements and needs—all served to create the framework for changes in service needs and requirements and competition in the 1990s. The major trends for this decade are discussed below.

Increased Technological Integration. New developments in extremely high density integrated microprocessor circuitry and data storage will continue to significantly improve mean time between failures (MTBF) and equipment reliability in high levels of system integration. These factors and the decreasing cost of built-in diagnostics will lead to increased modularity and a full commitment to "pull-and-replace" servicing as opposed to fixing in the field. The continuing evolution of microprocessor technology will lead to ever-increasing processor speeds and capabilities at lower and lower costs. This highly integrated technology will be applied in a much broader array of products and systems—including building automation and process control, plant automation, medical electronics instrumentation, and even high-voltage switchgear and power distribution equipment—as VLSI-based* microchips replace PLCs* in process control and building automation and as digital circuits, ISDNs,* and fiber optics replace analog and twisted-pair circuitry in voice telecommunications.

The dimensions of the service engineer's task will be affected as the newer technology makes increasing use of data-oriented, microprocessor modules for controls in electromechanical and even mechanical environments. The service engineer will become more of a service manager, responsible for coordinating and delivering service rather than depot repair. Service in the low-tech markets will also change; service personnel will have to deal with the total customer needs and requirements. This means that the service person must become much more sensitive to customers' service requirements—proactively identifying and resolving problems rather than waiting for complaints to arrive.

Increased Networking. Another major development in the high-tech markets is the increasing trend toward integrated networks based on open systems architecture and interface standards. Even though the battle over which particular interface standard will ultimately apply will continue in the 1990s, it is quite clear that there is a broad industry commitment to the multivendor open systems environment. Thus not only will the basic trend toward networking continue, but service organizations will need the capability to fully service both stand-alone products and the network interfaces, the switches, and the network technology. Again, there are implications for service in the general market: the need to extend service beyond the framework of the product to the customer's full environment.

Increased Focus on Service Quality and Standards. The growing installed base of technology and the increasing dependence of users on that technology will continue to lead customers to increase their focus on service quality on a stand-alone basis. In the past, customers were willing to allow the product vendors to establish their own service stan-

---

*VLSI stands for *very large scale integration*. PLCs are *program logic controllers*. ISDN stands for *Integrated Services Digital Network*.

dards; today, the users' growing dependence on technology is creating a greater awareness of the impact of service quality and service delivery. Also, the rising cost of an internal maintenance staff is leading many user organizations to reduce internal maintenance and support staffs by increasingly contracting out service responsibilities. Service quality is therefore becoming of paramount importance.

In the United Kingdom, for example, the British Standards Institution (BSI), in conjunction with the United Kingdom Chapter of the Association of Field Service Managers International (AFSMI), has taken the lead in developing specific standards for quality in high-tech service. (These standards are known as BS-5750.) The concept of service quality is now being developed by the International Standards Organization (ISO) under ISO-9000 as a framework for general use. In the automobile industry, customer satisfaction surveys by J. D. Powers & Associates are becoming a standard by which the industry measures quality.

It is clear that service quality has become an issue of growing importance. Thus standards of service quality will continue to be developed and used for judging service performance.

Increased Commitment to Service as a Strategic Differentiator. The fourth major trend, which will be accelerated by a focus on service quality from both the vendor and user communities, is an increasing commitment to a strategic service management approach. This is due to the maturing of technology coupled with the increased competition, leading to a growing array of product features and capabilities at decreasing prices.

The increased impact of downtime will lead potential customers to view service as the primary strategic differentiator between vendor offers. At the same time, decreasing profit margins for products and maturing product life cycles will lead vendors to recognize the strategic value of service as both a mechanism for market penetration and market control and a direct source of revenues and profits. These combined customer and vendor pressures on management will lead to a greater commitment to service as both an independent profit center and a strategic line of business.

Improved Service Management Systems and Technology. Finally, the service technology vendors will become increasingly committed to providing a broader array of technology and systems designed specifically for improving service productivity and meeting growing service management needs and requirements. This commitment from vendors will stem from the increasing focus on service management by service and corporate-level executives and the growing recognition of the strategic importance of service and the high return on investment from service.

The broad array of integrated technology will include field service management system software that can operate on mainframes, minicomputers, and microprocessors.

The increasing availability of artificial intelligence technology for service diagnostics and maintenance support will give service a more capital-intensive and less labor-driven orientation. Hand-held terminals, utilizing on-line FM or cellular radio and featuring high-density storage and retrieval and high-density video displays, will be available in portable or lap-top form for use by service engineers in the field. These terminals will improve communications between service managers at headquarters and service engineers in the field, as well as enhance the ability of the service engineers (at the repair sites) to rapidly diagnose problems and order parts. New integrated technology for logistics management and control and forecasting will also become increasingly available and will be standardized. This improved technology for service management, delivery, and control will further improve the economies of scale and increase the capital intensity of service operations.

Future Impact of Major Long-Term Trends

The major trends discussed above will change the dimensions and structure of service management and service organization, as well as operating concepts. Preparing for these changes is an essential element of the service executive's job. The major predicted impacts are explained below.

Management of Service as a Full Strategic Line of Business. The elevation of service to a strategic line of business places increasing demands on both the service organization and the service executive's role and responsibilities. Typically, both the content of a service portfolio and service prices were dictated by the marketing and sales organization. The operation of service as a strategic line of business requires that service executives establish a strategic planning and marketing staff of their own, focusing on the special requirements for marketing, merchandising, and selling service and the establishment of service prices. Since the typical service manager or executive has not been trained in market-related issues, it is clear that the caliber of service executives will have to improve in this particular critical dimension. Perhaps even more important is the need for service executives to establish the structure and conceptual outlook required to operate service strategically as one of the critical "legs" of the corporate business base.

Increased Centralization and Growth in Service Organization Size and Capabilities. New technologies for call handling and dispatch, call avoidance, and logistics control, as well as greater opportunities for improving economies of scale, will increase the need for centralization, particularly for call handling and logistics control. Service organizations will continue to grow larger through mergers, acquisitions, and internal expansion. This growth will broaden the portfolio of services to include depot repair, parts supply, and training, as well as an array of newer services and capabilities, including systems integration, software support, catastrophic backup, installation, moves, upgrades, and expansion.

Increased Emphasis on Vertical Market Segmentation. Perhaps one of the most important impacts that will occur in the 1990s is the increase in sophistication and commitment with regard to service marketing and sales. Historically, the marketing and sales functions for service were generally handled with a highly focused product orientation. Vertical market segmentation (the focus on the service needs of individual classes of customers such as banks, hospitals, high-tech manufacturing firms, and government), which has been the hallmark of the maturing product business, will begin to take place in service as the service organizations recognize that the great profit and growth opportunities lie primarily in "servicing" classes of *customers* rather than *products.*

The trend toward running service as a strategic line of business will increase the adoption and use of advanced marketing concepts, including market research, value-in-use pricing, and improved advertising and merchandising of the newly emerging, broadened service portfolio, with a greater focus on key vertical market segments characterized by high density and a high value in use for service. This focus on vertical or user-oriented market segments will accelerate as service organizations begin to make more effective use of strategic partnering: entering into continuing working relationships with other service organizations in order to provide a single point of contact for a given class of customers.

Electronic Augmentation of the Field Service Engineer. The significant improvements which will take place in the development and implementation of high-density, extremely lightweight processing, storage, and retrieval technology, coupled with the increasing need of the service engineer to be able to support a broad variety of technology and equipment at the customer's location, will lead to a very significant increase in the technology deployed to support the individual field service engineer. The typical service engineer of the 1990s will be equipped with a full, portable test and support system, essentially a micro service management system, which will provide, through a high-density video display, access to complete diagnostic test and repair data based upon information keyed through an alphanumeric pad to an on-board processor. Test probes, linked through the portable device to central processors, will provide the full capability for diagnostic tests at the circuit board and subassembly level. Finally, full voice recognition capabilities within the hand-held terminal will facilitate on-line reporting of both service call information and parts use.

The electronically equipped service engineers of the future will be capable of fixing a much broader array of equipment, and through on-line, real-time connections to central headquarters, technical assistance centers, and logistics centers, they will be provided with complete support in terms of both technical knowledge and parts. The introduction of direct couriers and roving delivery vans will further improve the ability to deliver parts to customer sites and thus reduce the number of "broken" service calls. Finally, the employment of artificial intelligence (AI) technology for call avoidance in the call-handling function will significantly reduce the number of on-site service calls required, and the use of the same AI technology within the hand-held, portable terminals in the field will improve the diagnostics utilized as part of the repair process.

The service engineer will become more professional and increasingly concerned about the management of the full service environment of the customer, as opposed to the current focus on individual products and stand-alone technology. In essence, the increasingly sophisticated customer, focusing on service quality in a multivendor network environment, will demand a more mature and sophisticated service engineer, one who is capable of performing the broad array of tasks required to fully serve customers in their operating environment.

Globalization of Service Management and Delivery. The increasing deployment of technology on a worldwide basis, as well as the general trend toward reducing trade barriers and constraints, will also create a very strong requirement for a global, strategic view of service management and control. Historically, service was managed on a country-by-country basis because of border or customs regulations and significant differences in culture and the physical structure of the business environment. Some firms are already reorganizing to meet the long-term requirement of a total international approach to service management, control, and delivery.

It is clear that a total global approach to service will include worldwide logistics support and the integrated use of reliability, maintainability, and failure data to improve diagnostics and forecasting accuracy.

This will result in a significant change in inventory and stocking mechanisms and will lead to a true, just-in-time inventory control and management system on a worldwide basis.

We will see the emergence of major corporate organizations offering a total service capability that has naturally evolved from operating service as a strategic line of business. This strategic focus on service allows growth in both revenues and profits without dependence on product manufacturing. The maturing service economies of the 1990s will require the emergence of major corporate forces capable of meeting the growing mix of service needs and requirements of the industrial, commercial, and consumer markets.

Summary

The major trends over the last decade will create significant changes in the 1990s. In addition, major events that can be observed at least on the immediate horizon, including the growing acceptance of new integrated telecommunications technology and the planned initiatives which will form a great new market throughout Europe in the post-1992 era, will create the environment for future change. Service organizations that continue to conduct business as usual, focusing primarily on a limited set of customer services and operating on a decentralized basis, will find the shock of more aggressive competitors and changing customer requirements and needs to be quite severe. I strongly urge that service executives seriously consider the changing dimensions of the market, including the growing needs of key vertical market segments, the growing international nature of service, and the broadening array of technology and systems for more effective management and control of service operations. By evaluating both the trends discussed above and the predicted impacts, service executives can position their organization to take advantage of the revolutionary changes which will occur in the service industry.

Appendix **A**

Economic, Legal, and Logical Arguments for Support of Independent Service Organizations

General Issues

There are a number of strong economic and logical arguments as to why manufacturers should support independent service organizations. In the first place, users and potential users of equipment strongly indicate that a critical factor in the decision to buy a product from a vendor is the availability of quality and cost-effective service for that product. Thus it logically follows that the greater the number of qualified service organizations available for a particular class of equipment, the greater will be the product demand.

In addition, since users are increasingly demanding a single point of contact for service and many manufacturers are reluctant to provide fully integrated service, it follows that it is to the advantage of any one manufacturer to ensure that the new vendors offering total, integrated service are capable of servicing the firm's particular product. Obviously, the best strategy for an equipment vendor is to provide a full range of integrated services on an independent basis—i.e., to separate services from product offerings to give the customer a full choice of either products or services or both.

A service manager may be given the responsibility for a full customer site, thus becoming the total-service agent for a particular user. The service prices for equipment that the manager cannot directly service or support may then be higher than the normal market prices, reflecting the additional costs of subcontracting and service coordination. A service manager may also encourage the user to replace the equipment which the service organization is not supporting with the equipment of a vendor who is willing to provide the service manager with support in the long run. Thus the increasing demand from users for a *single service manager* to service all equipment in the establishment will force more and more manufacturers to rely on independent service organizations to provide service, including parts, logistics support, and even technical assistance.

The long-term trend in the market is toward this approach. This is particularly true in market segments where viable, credible independent service managers have begun to appear and offer services that have been *demonstrated* to be highly responsive, cost-effective, and comprehensive. My market research clearly shows that an *increasing* number of users are interested in buying service independently of products, from organizations offering *both* products or technology *and* service.

Manufacturers, in the long run, will be *forced by their customers* to offer service as a separate line of business to the market. This will reduce the opportunity for a full tie-in between service and product and will potentially eliminate any direct profit margin advantages which might accrue as a result of withholding parts, documentation, training, and refurbishment capability from independent service organizations.

Legal Arguments and Issues in the Service Market

In addition to the economic and logical arguments I have already presented, there are other trends which may force manufacturers to support independent service organizations. These are based on an increasing number of legal actions designed to test the question of the manufacturer's rights versus independent service organization rights. The legal actions stem from alleged violations with respect to the Sherman Antitrust Act, the Clayton Act, the Robinson Patman Act, fair trade practices, patent issues, defamation, etc. Table A-1 presents a general list of manufacturer strategies for withholding support from independent service organizations and possible legal arguments which can be used by independent service organizations to oppose those strategies. The manufacturer strategies include taking legal actions to protect software, using corporate law, and providing different levels of support.

There are a number of current cases with respect to the legal questions involved in the servicing and support of electronic products. These current legal actions are all attempts to resolve the question of whether or not manufacturers can withhold parts, documentation, training, and other support services from independent service organizations on a legal basis. The resolution of this issue in the courts will ultimately depend upon the definition and existence of an independent, relevant market structure for service and the determination of whether or not an individual manufacturer, by withholding service and support, has created a monopoly position or is engaging in unfair trade practices.

An operational question facing both the manufacturer and the independent service supplier in these legal actions concerns the *size and structure of the relevant service market.* An important issue in developing a legal argument is whether a market exists (consisting of customers demanding specific types of service and suppliers of those types of service) which is separate and distinguishable from other markets—either product markets or other service markets. If the specific service market is independent and one organization is handling a very high percentage of total service requirements, that organization may be regarded as a monopolist and may be restrained from certain actions such as withholding parts or technical diagnostics.

The general trend suggests that service is becoming an increasingly independent market, separable from related product markets, in that customers, presented with options, are choosing service vendors independently of their product vendors. A further analysis of these emerging manufacturer-based service markets requires more critical evaluation: Can the service provider in one market easily threaten skills and resources in another? The greater the degree of separability and independence, the greater the number of opportunities for applying legal measures such as the Sherman Antitrust Act, the Clayton Act, or the Robinson Patman Act against manufacturers' actions to control or inhibit independent service providers, or third-party maintainers, in a specific service market.

While we have to wait for the resolution of the electronics industry cases in the courts, we can look at a similar set of cases which were settled within the last few years. These cases concerned the servicing and

Table A-1. Potential Legal Arguments for Opposing Manufacturer Strategies against Independent Service Organizations

Manufacturer strategy	Potential arguments	Issues
Protect software procedures or practices on the basis of copyright.	Title 17 of U.S. Code, Section 17, which provides limitations on exclusive rights for computer programs: "It is not an infringement for the owner of a copy of a computer program to make or authorize the making of another copy," provided that "such a new copy is created as an essential step in the utilization of the computer program in conjunction with a machine." Also see Title 17 of U.S. Code, Section 109.	The use of software by service organizations: Is utilization essential? Is the service organization an agent of the owner?
Withhold parts, documentation, and diagnostics from independent service firms to protect related service market.	Section 2 of the Sherman Antitrust Act, which prevents monopolization or attempts to monopolize in the market	What is the relevant market? Is the manufacturer engaged in willful, purposeful conduct? Is a monopoly posture acquired legitimately or by exercise of intention or innovation?
Provide support for various service organizations differently, in an attempt to create an advantage or control selected markets.	Section 1 of the Sherman Antitrust Act, which prevents conspiracy or collaboration in restraint of trade Robinson Patman Act, which prevents treating similar organizations differently	Proof of the following is required: Price fixing Division of markets Tying arrangements

Table A-1. Potential Legal Arguments for Opposing Manufacturer Strategies against Independent Service Organizations (*Continued*)

Manufacturer strategy	Potential arguments	Issues
Use marketing, sales, and technical forces to reduce confidence of customers in ability of independent service organization to perform.	Variety of laws on: Intentional interference with business Unfair competition Disparagement and defamation	Proof of the following is required: Damages Specifications
Change, without appropriate notice or negotiations, support policies and practices which affect the independent service organization's ability to perform.	Contract laws (breach of contract)	Proof of the following is required: Contract form and structure Extent of damages
Tie, or link, different types of service and support to provide a total service package for a customer.	Clayton Act, which prohibits tying through the use of monopoly position or changing tying relationships to restrain trade	Are the services tied for technical or efficiency reasons? Is a monopoly position used to create tying relationships?

support of heating, ventilation, and air-conditioning (HVAC) controls in the U.S. market. Contractors involved in the installation and servicing of HVAC controls manufactured by Trane, Carrier, and other companies attempted to resolve this issue in the courts. The cases ultimately were settled by the participants themselves (without final resolution in the courts) in favor of the service contractors. Individual agreements between each manufacturer and the contractors now provide the independent service organizations with access to parts and other support requirements. This experience suggests that the question of the ability of manufacturers to withhold parts, documentation, training, and other support services from independent service organizations will be resolved in favor of the independent service organizations—in cases in which such actions are deemed a monopolization of trade or an infringement of fair trade practices.

In the United Kingdom, similar legal questions were also considered within the last few years. In one case, automobile manufacturers attempted to stop the suppliers of parts from selling them indiscriminately in the aftermarket on the grounds of patent infringement. That case was resolved in favor of the parts suppliers. More recently, in a case involving DPCE, a major third-party maintenance firm, and ICL, a major computer manufacturer, the ruling was that ICL must make available its error-logging and diagnostic support software for its VME operating system. In general, the existing legal arguments tend to support the independent service providers, particularly where there is evidence that the manufacturer is engaging in monopolistic or unfair trade practices or is attempting to control the service aftermarket.

Summary

Independent service organizations interested in expanding their role and position in the market and concerned with strategic attempts by manufacturers to withhold parts, diagnostics, training, and other support services should recognize that there is a growing economic and logical rationale, and potentially even legal precedent, which militates against such a strategy. Independent service organizations should recognize the existence of a broad base of legal regulations designed to thwart manufacturers' attempts to monopolize service activities.

Manufacturers engaged in such practices should seriously reconsider their position with respect to their support of, and cooperation with, independent service organizations. Under any circumstances, they should ensure that their actions are not in violation of Sections 1 and 2 of the Sherman Antitrust Act; Title 17, Section 17, of the U.S. Code; or the variety of laws relating to unfair trade practices, interference with business, etc.

My analysis indicates that in the *long run*, it is probably to the disadvantage of manufacturers to withhold parts, documentation, training, and other support services from independent service organizations. In fact, offering these to qualified independent service organizations *at a standard price* should lead to a significant increase in revenues and profits from product sales and services (supplies) sales, as well as an expansion of the general service industry to support each individual manufacturer's product lines. Consequently, the general market acceptance of the individual manufacturer's products will be enhanced, and market share will improve. Manufacturers attempting to capture a major share of the service market can best achieve this goal by creating a strategic, independent service business and delivering *high-quality services* directly to the relevant service market on a competitive basis, independent of product lines.

In the *short run*, an alternative approach might be best for the manufacturers if they want to protect their service revenues and profit base. This desire would, of course, be limited by the extent of their control of the market. If, in fact, they are truly in a monopolistic position (i.e., they have significant market control), there may be certain specific constraints on their ability to unilaterally withhold parts, software support, diagnostics, etc. Thus the role of manufacturers relative to independent service organizations and third-party maintainers should be developed carefully and in accordance with legal advice.

Appendix **B**

The State of the Art in Standard Service Management Systems Software

Automation of the service management functions in manufacturer, distributor, and independent service organizations is a primary priority. Experience clearly indicates that service management systems can significantly improve service productivity, effectiveness, and delivery. While historically, automated service management systems often required lengthy and extremely expensive customized development, today's manager is faced with a real, cost-effective alternative. Over the last 8 years, a wide variety of standard software packages has been developed and successfully implemented. These standard *field service management systems* (FSMS) software packages provide integrated support of key service management functions and can economically support service operations ranging from 5 to 2500 or more service engineers.

Automated Field Service Management Functions

In general, the computerized field service management systems technology that has emerged in the field service industry is based on the major functions involved in the operation of the typical field service organization. The functions for which standard FSMS software has been developed include:

1. *Call handling and dispatch (CHAD)*, including limited diagnostic screening and technical assistance, as well as tracking and closing out of the service call

2. *Logistics management and control (LOG)*, including the entering and processing of orders for parts, inventory tracking and control, and the scheduling and control of repairs

3. *Database management (DATA)*, including standard and ad hoc reporting

4. *Financial and administrative management (FIN)*, to ensure the receipt of full revenues for services rendered (e.g., warranty and contract services) and some level of *financial control* of the revenue and cost components of service operations

In essence, the development of individual, customized systems has now resulted in an array of standardized, transferable software packages. The general structure of typical FSMS software has been influenced by the growing importance of maintenance and service within national and international companies and by the rapid changes in computer and communications technology.

Available Field Service Management Systems Software

A number of integrated, automated field service management systems have been developed and implemented over the last 2 or 3 years and are currently being merchandised to the field service community in the United States and Canada. More than 20 firms currently provide FSMS technology. The available standard software packages include:

- Alert system (Alert Computer Systems, Inc.)
- Applause™ and Depot Repair™ (Xcel Computer Systems, Inc.)
- Class (Customation, Inc.)
- Computerized Maintenance Management System®, or COMMS® (Patton Consultants, Inc.)
- Concert (Micro Design, Inc.)
- Controlcomp (Verticomp)
- Crossroads (Giant Technology, Inc.)
- Cymbol/Cornerstone (Captiva Computer Services)

- Dispatch Control (Combustioneer Software Services, Inc.)
- Dispatch-1 (Applied Systems Technology, Inc.)
- FACS [Florida Air Conditioning Systems (FACS)]
- Fastrak (Core Software, Inc.)
- Fieldforce (Pyramid Technology Corporation)
- Fieldmain (DSA Systems)
- Fieldwatch™ and Microfieldwatch™ (Data Group Corporation)
- Manman/Serviceman (ASK Computer Systems, Inc.)
- S-2000 (Service Systems International, Ltd.)
- Service Edge® (DNS Associates, Inc.)
- Service Management System (Ultimate Southern California)
- Servicetrak (Active Software, Inc.)
- SIMS (Sidon Solutions Corporation)
- Super Service and Micro Super Service (Pacific Decision Sciences Corporation)
- Uptime® (Minicomputer Software Specialists, Inc.)

A full list of software vendors is shown in Table B-1. A full review and evaluation was made of the software packages listed above to identify those which support the key functions of call handling and dispatch, logistics control, and database management *and* have been implemented in one or more service organizations. The standard FSMS software packages which meet these criteria are listed in Table B-2. These software packages all provide the capability for call handling and dispatch, logistics support, and database management. Many also provide some additional capabilities for financial control, invoicing, planning, and forecasting. Software is available for large minicomputers and mainframes such as IBM and DEC (e.g., Super Service, Fieldwatch, and Dispatch-1), for minicomputers such as Prime and Data General (Service Edge, COMMS, and Super Service), and for microcomputers and PCs (Concert, COMMS, Micro Super Service, and Dispatch-1). As shown in Table B-3, prices for basic FSMS software range from about $200,000 to less than $1000, depending on the functionality, type of computer, and vendor. The newest developments include microprocessor-based software packages which have fully integrated capabilities and which can be networked to allow for modular growth as required. Vendor addresses and sales contacts are listed in Table B-4.

Table B-1. Major Suppliers of FSMS Software

An Overview

Supplier	Software	Installation status	Comments
Active Software, Inc.	Servicetrak	800 systems	A micro/PC LAN-based, fully integrated package supporting all basic functions, with many enhancements available
Alert Computer Systems, Inc.	Alert system	100 systems installed	Fully integrated field service management information system that supports call handling and dispatch, inventory, contract administration, repair, order processing, and additional functions Also available as a stand-alone system
Applied Systems Technology, Inc.	Dispatch-1	275 systems installed	Combines service management functions with bill of materials, inventory, and accounting systems to cover a wide range of requirements of service organizations
ASK Computer Systems, Inc.	Manman/Serviceman	112 systems	Supports all the functional areas necessary to maintain the effectiveness and profitability of a field service organization
Captiva Computer Services	Cymbol/Cornerstone	NA*	FSMS software suite which supports all core FSMS functions
Combustioneer Software Services, Inc.	Dispatch Control	< 5 systems	In-house FSMS software brought to market Provides basic functions, including call handling, scheduling, accounting, and a level of inventory control
Core Software, Inc.	Fastrak	300 complete systems	A series of integrated packages written in Dataflex Designed to support all the functional areas necessary to maintain a relatively small staffed field service organization

Company	Product	Number of systems	Description
Customation, Inc.	Class	8 systems	Supports call handling and dispatch, with some inventory control included; Profitability and productivity reports are also produced; includes a call-avoidance subsystem; A well-designed product designed to run in a minicomputer environment
Data Group Corporation	Fieldwatch™ Microfieldwatch™	185 systems 20 systems	One of the top three integrated FSMS software products; Four new options available in 1988; Optional hand-held terminal interface; Available in mainframes and minicomputers
DNS Associates, Inc.	Service Edge®	6 systems	Supports the basic functions for managing a field service operation, such as call handling and dispatch, logistics, database management, and billing
DSA Systems	Fieldmain	NA	Supports all FSMS functions; Built upon 4GL DBMS technology; Written in Progress
Florida Air Conditioning Systems	FACS	410 systems	FSMS package designed to support HVAC, plumbing, and general contractors
Giant Technology, Inc.	Crossroads	NA	FSMS application built upon "real-world" accounting software
Micro Design, Inc.	Concert	84 systems	Integrated field service software designed for IBM XT/AT; Supports all standard functions
Minicomputer Software Specialists Inc.	Uptime®	10 systems	Provides specific features to deal with maintenance and service orders as well as associated call control and billing requirements; Operates on an HP-3000

Table B-1. Major Suppliers of FSMS Software (Continued)

Supplier	Software	Installation status	Comments
Pacific Decision Sciences Corporation	Super Service Micro Super Service	20 systems 1 system	A turnkey solution that supports call handling and dispatch, inventory, database management, and financial control Only software to support marketing users of a relational database
Patton Consultants, Inc.	COMMS® 10 COMMS® 20 COMMS® 30 COMMS® 40	30 systems	Software originally developed as an equipment maintenance system, but includes some of the functionality in traditional FSMS call handling and dispatch and inventory control COMMS® 10 and 20 software available to run on micros COMMS® 30 software available to run on minicomputers COMMS® 40 available via ORACLE DBMS
Pyramid Technology Corporation	Fieldforce	NA	UNIX-based FSMS package supplies core FSMS functions Presently available on Pyramid computers
Service Systems International, Ltd.	S-2000	170 systems	A system of fully integrated modules supporting all major functions
Sidon Solutions Corporation	SIMS	20 systems	Fully integrated management package Offers call control, inventory, and ledger systems
Ultimate Southern California	Service Management System	5 systems (est.)	Newly released to market in February 1988 Provides turnkey FSMS solutions
Verticomp	Controlcomp	NA	PICK-based FSMS package for distributors and general industry service operations
Xcel Computer Systems, Inc.	Applause™ Depot Repair™	62 systems 3 systems	A system of fully integrated modules built around a service database Has a number of features essential to a service organization

*NA = not available.

Table B-2. State-of-the-Art FSMS Software Packages in Use

Software	Company	Number of full customer systems installed*	Date of first installation (month/year)	Typical size of service organization (number of field engineers)	Language and/or operating system used	Equipment required (type and size)
Service Edge®	DNS Associates, Inc.	6	01/86	20–2000	Transact and Fortran	Any Prime computer
Super Service	Pacific Decision Sciences Corporation	20	06/82	25–unlimited	RPG, EDMS, or UNIX	Microdata, Prime, Ultimate, DEC, IBM
Super Service/ IBM	Pacific Decision Sciences Corporation	4	06/84	15–200	RPG, EDMS, or UNIX	IBM 36 and 38, Wang
Micro Super Service	Pacific Decision Sciences Corporation	1	NA†	5–20	RPG, EDMS, or UNIX	IBM PC compatibles, IBM 36/PC
Uptime®	Minicomputer Software Specialists, Inc.	10	06/84	40+	Cobol	HP-3000, any model
Dispatch-1	Applied Systems Technology, Inc.	275	08/84	2–unlimited	Progress, UNIX, XENIX, MS-DOS	IBM PC through DEC VAX 1180
Fieldwatch™	Data Group Corporation	Approx. 200	08/80	5–2500	Cobol	IBM 43XX, 30XX; DEC—all VAX series; HP minis
COMMS® 10 and 20	Patton Consultants, Inc.	None	NA	100–150	dBASE II Plus, Novell network	IBM AT/XT or compatibles

Table B-2. State-of-the-Art FSMS Software Packages in Use (Continued)

Software	Company	Number of full customer systems installed*	Date of first installation (month/year)	Typical size of service organization (number of field engineers)	Language and/or operating system used	Equipment required (type and size)
COMMS® 30 COMMS® 40	Patton Consultants, Inc.	30	01/80	20–unlimited	Cobol	Data General MV series, IBM S/36, Honeywell
Concert	Micro Design, Inc.	84	NA	5–200	Novell network, MS-DOS	IBM AT/XT clones, 30 MB
SIMS	Sidon Solutions Corporation	20	10/84	15–300	PICK	All PICK-compatible minis
Alert system	Alert Computer Systems, Inc.	100	02/82	1–unlimited	PICK	Any PICK-compatible
Applause™	Xcel Computer Systems, Inc.	62	03/86	100	Pascal, DBMS	Macintosh 512, Macintosh Plus
Depot Repair™	Xcel Computer Systems, Inc.	3	09/86	12	Pascal, DBMS	Macintosh 512, Macintosh Plus
Field Facts™	Soft Solutions	6	06/85	35–560+	RPG II	IBM 34, 36
Micro Field Facts™	Soft Solutions			10–50	RPG II	IBM PC compatibles
Manman/ Serviceman	ASK Computer Systems, Inc.	112	02/83	5–unlimited	VMS, MPE	DEC VAX, HP-3000
Class	Customation, Inc.	8	06/82	5–unlimited	VMS, RMS	DEC VAX, Datapoint

Product	Company	Number Installed*	Date	Users	Software/OS (Dataflex, XENIX, UNIX V, VMS)	Hardware (Multiuser micros, NCR Tower, DEC VAX)
Fastrak	Core Software, Inc.	300	11/84	10–30	Dataflex, XENIX, UNIX V, VMS	Multiuser micros, NCR Tower, DEC VAX
S-2000	Service Systems International, Ltd.	170	08/83	5–unlimited	MS-DOS, RPG II	IBM PC; IBM 36, 38
Cymbol/Cornerstone	Captiva Computer Services	NA	NA	5–unlimited	NA	Tandem
Crossroads	Giant Technology, Inc.	NA	NA	5–1000	UNIX, XENIX, MS-DOS	Various micro-computers
Dispatch Control	Combustioneer Software Services, Inc.	< 5	NA	5–100	RPG II	IBM 34/36XX
FACS	Florida Air Conditioning Systems	410	NA	5–50	UNIX	Altos, Northern Telecom
Servicetrak	Active Software, Inc.	800	01/87	1–unlimited	DOS 3.1, 2.1	IBM PC/AT/XT, PS/2
Service Management System	Ultimate Southern California		02/88	5–300	NA	Various IBM minis and micros
Fieldforce	Pyramid Technology Corporation	NA	NA	NA	UNIX	Pyramid
Controlcomp	Verticomp	NA	NA	1–250	PICK	PICK-compatible
Fieldmain	DSA Systems	NA	NA	5–unlimited	Progress	Any Progress-compatible hardware

*Multiple systems installed for one customer are regarded as *one* system.
†NA = not available.

Table B-3. Price Ranges of Standard FSMS Software

Software	Base price	Typical price	Hardware
		Mainframes and Large Minisystems	
Fieldwatch™	$120,000	$350,000	IBM 43XX, 30XX; DEC VAX
Super Service	$140,000	$200,000	Microdata, IBM 43XX, DEC VAX, and others
COMMS® 30 and 40	$ 79,000	$150,000	Data General MV series, Honeywell, IBM S/36, ORACLE-compatible
Dispatch-1	$150,000	$300,000	DEC VAX 1180
Uptime®	$ 25,000	$ 35,000	HP-3000
Alert system	$217,000	$300,000	Any PICK-compatible
Manman/Serviceman	$ 55,000	$145,000	DEC VAX, HP-3000
		Small to Medium Minisystems	
Field Facts™	$ 44,500	$ 52,500	IBM 34, 36
Service Edge®	$ 35,000	$ 70,000	Prime
Super Service	$ 30,000	$ 50,000	IBM 36, 38; Wang
Uptime®	$ 25,000	$ 35,000	HP-3000
Alert system	$100,000	$110,000	Any PICK-compatible mini
Fieldwatch™	$ 45,000	$140,000	DEC VAX, HP minis
SIMS	$ 30,000	$ 40,000	All PICK-compatible minis
Dispatch-1	NA*	NA	Various HP and DEC minis, IBM-compatible micros
COMMS® 30 and 40	$ 39,000	$ 79,000	Data General MV series, ORACLE-compatible

Class	$15,000	$35,000	DEC VAX, Datapoint
Fastrak	$ 1,800	$ 9,000	DEC VAX, NCR Tower
S-2000	$25,000	$40,000	IBM 36, 38
FACS	NA	NA	Altos, Northern Telecom
Concord	NA	NA	IBM 34, 36
Dispatch Control	NA	NA	IBM 34, 36
Service Management System	NA	NA	Various minis, IBM micros
Microcomputers and Personal Computers			
Microfieldwatch™	$ 4,000	$ 7,000	IBM PC clone, DEC VAX, HP
COMMS® 10 and 20	$ 8,900	$12,900	IBM PC, AT/XT clones
Concert	$ 6,700	$10,000	IBM AT/XT clones
Dispatch-1	$ 4,500	$10,000	IBM AT/XT
Micro Super Service	$15,000	$25,000	IBM PC and AT compatibles, IBM S/36
Applause™	$ 6,500	$12,000	Macintosh 512, Plus; IBM PCs
Depot Repair™	$ 1,500	1,500	Macintosh 512, Plus
Micro Field Facts™	$13,500	$16,500	IBM PC and compatibles
Fastrak	$ 1,800	$ 9,000	Multiuser micros
S-2000	$ 5,000	$ 8,000	IBM PC
Servicetrak	$ 795	$ 2,375	IBM PC/AT/XT, PS/2

*NA = not available.

Table B-4. Companies That Offer FSMS Software

Company name	Address	Telephone	Name of software package(s)	Key sales contact
Active Software, Inc.	1208 Apollo Way, Suite 507 Sunnyvale, CA 94086	(408) 732-1740	Servicetrak	Anthony Samfilippo
Alert Computer Systems, Inc.	1708-G Southeast Main Street Irvine, CA 92714	(714) 261-9366	Alert system	Mike Ryan
Applied System Technology, Inc.	100 High Point Drive Chalfont, PA 18914	(215) 822-8888	Dispatch-1	Ilene DeJong
ASK Computer Systems, Inc.	2440 El Camino Real West Mountain View, CA 94040	(415) 696-4442	Manman/Serviceman	Randy Heatter
Captiva Computer Services	6390 LBJ Freeway, St. 150 Dallas, TX 75240	(214) 387-5678	Cymbol/Cornerstone	Chris Smith
Combustioneer Software Services, Inc.	645A Loftstrand Lane Rockville, MD 20850	(301) 340-2290	Dispatch Control	—
Core Software, Inc.	26303 Oak Ridge Drive Spring, TX 77380	(713) 292-2177	Fastrak	Cindy Mathieu
Customation, Inc.	629 Amboy Avenue Edison, NJ 08837	(201) 738-4755	Class	Bob Hearns

Company	Address	Phone	Product	Contact
Data Group Corporation (subsidiary of NYNEX)	77 South Bedford Street Burlington, MA 01830	(617) 272-4100	Fieldwatch™ Microfieldwatch™	Charles Fohlin
DNS Associates, Inc.	1762 Massachusetts Avenue Lexington, MA 02173	(617) 862-8564	Service Edge®	Jim Newkirk
DSA Systems	Box C2, Deer Crossing, Rte. 28 Mashpee, MA 02649	(508) 477-2540	Fieldmain	David Smith
Florida Air Conditioning Systems	6491 Powers Avenue Jacksonville, FL 32217	(904) 739-0822	FACS	Liz Baron
Giant Technology, Inc.	714 South Charles Street Baltimore, MD 21230	(301) 685-2223	Crossroads	Toni Frank
Micro Design, Inc.	509 Benjamin Fox Pavillion Jenkintown, PA 19406	(215) 884-1112	Concert	—
Minicomputer Software Specialists, Inc.	200 Executive Drive Brookfield, WI 53005	(414) 784-5575	Uptime®	Noel Cooley
Pacific Decision Sciences Corporation	12345 Newport Avenue Santa Ana, CA 92705	(714) 832-2200	Super Service Micro Super Service Super Service/IBM	Hark Vasa
Patton Consultants, Inc.	3699 West Henrietta Road Rochester, NY 14623	(716) 334-2554	COMMS® 10 COMMS® 20 COMMS® 30 COMMS® 40	George Doremus

Table B-4. Companies That Offer FSMS Software (Continued)

Company name	Address	Telephone	Name of software package(s)	Key sales contact
Pyramid Technology Corporation	1295 Charleston Road Mountain View, CA 94039	(415) 965-7200	Fieldforce	Kevin Smith
Service Systems International, Ltd.	219 Perimeter Center Parkway Suite 303, Atlanta, GA 30346	(404) 395-1133	S-2000	Roger Robertson
Sidon Solutions Corporation	8907 Warner Avenue Huntington Beach, CA 92647	(714) 848-4850	SIMS	Kevin Halvorson
Ultimate Southern California	1063 McGraw Avenue Irvine, CA 92714	(714) 280-3222	Service Management System	—
Verticomp	6 Courthouse Lane Chelmsford, MA 01824	(508) 458-3458	Controlcomp (field service operations)	Larry Traver
Xcel Computer Systems, Inc.	10 Mechanic Street Worcester, MA 01608	(617) 799-9494	Applause® Depot Repair® First Step Contract Generation Quotation Preparation Budget Prep®	Joseph DiPilato

Summary

Significant developments have taken place with respect to field service management systems software packages which have been designed to support service operations on an integrated basis. These software packages are now available for mainframes, such as the IBM 30XX and the large DEC VAX; for miniprocessors, such as Data General and Prime; and for personal computers and microprocessors, such as the IBM PC, the IBM XT, and Hewlett-Packard equipment. A number of standard software packages now exist which can be utilized by service organizations to support the rapid development of advanced service management systems and the implementation of these systems in their respective operations.

It should be noted that the lists of vendor products and prices in the tables were accurate at the time this book was prepared (fall of 1989). Readers are advised to contact vendors directly to obtain up-to-the-minute operating characteristics and prices for specific products.

Bibliography

General Books on Service Trends

Albrecht, Karl: *At America's Service*, Dow Jones–Irwin, Homewood, Ill., 1988.
Albrecht, Karl, and Ron Zemke: *Service America*, Dow Jones–Irwin, Homewood, Ill., 1985.
Heskett, James L.: *Managing in the Service Economy*, Harvard Business School Press, Boston, Mass., 1986.

Service Operations Management

Chase, R. B., and N. J. Aquilano: *Production and Operations Management*, Irwin, Homewood, Ill., 1981.
Lovelock, Christopher: *Service Marketing*, Prentice-Hall, Englewood Cliffs, N.J., 1984.
Norman, Richard: *Service Management: Strategy and Leadership in Service Business*, John Wiley & Sons, New York, 1986.
Sasser, W. E., R. P. Olsen, and D. D. Wyckoff: *Management of Service Operations*, Allyn and Bacon, Boston, 1978.
Voss, Armistead, Johnston, and Morris: *Operations Management in Service Industries and the Public Sector*, John Wiley & Sons, New York, 1985.
Wild, R.: *Concepts for Operations Management*, John Wiley & Sons, Chichester, England, 1977.

Queueing Theory

Cooper, R. B.: *Introduction to Queueing Theory*, Macmillan, New York, 1972.
Gross, D., and C. M. Harris: *Fundamentals of Queueing Theory*, John Wiley & Sons, New York, 1974.
Kleinrock, L.: *Queueing Systems*, vol. I: *Theory*, John Wiley & Sons, New York, 1979.
Kleinrock, L.: *Queueing Systems*, vol. II: *Computer Applications*, John Wiley & Sons, New York, 1979.

Reliability Theory

Green, A. E., and A. J. Bourne: *Reliability Technology*, Wiley Interscience, New York, 1973.
Lloyd, D. K., and M. Lipow: *Reliability: Management Methods and Mathematics*, Prentice-Hall, Englewood Cliffs, N.J., 1962.
Shooman, M. L.: *Probabilistic Reliability: An Engineering Approach*, McGraw-Hill, New York, 1968.

Inventory Systems

Hadley, G., and T. M. Within: *Analysis of Inventory Systems*, Prentice-Hall, Englewood Cliffs, N.J., 1963.
Lewis, C. D.: *Scientific Inventory Control*, American Elsevier, New York, 1970.
Wight, O. W.: *Production and Inventory Management in the Computer Age*, Cahners Books, Boston, 1974.

Index

About the Author

Donald F. Blumberg is the founder and president of D. F. Blumberg & Associates, Inc., a Ft. Washington, Pennsylvania–based management consulting firm specializing in the development and implementation of service strategies for some of the nation's major data processing, office automation, telecommunications, and medical electronics corporations. He is a pioneer in viewing service as a strategic mechanism for improving market and product share and generating revenue and profit margins. Mr. Blumberg has served as a consultant on service strategy planning, market research, and productivity improvement for more than 500 corporations in North America, Europe, and the Far East.

Prior to founding D. F. Blumberg & Associates, Inc., Mr. Blumberg served as the director of strategic planning and operations research at Philco-Ford, where he developed innovative service strategies for one of the largest technical services organizations in the United States. Mr. Blumberg earned his B.A. degree from the University of Pennsylvania and his M.A. from the Wharton School of Business.